Praise for

RIDING THROUGH GRIEF

Riding Through Grief offers hope and helpful insight to others trying to find their way through the loss of a loved one. It will be a valuable resource for family members and friends who accompany these individuals on their journeys, as well as for mental health and other health care professionals seeking more effective ways to help people experiencing such a loss. . . . It is an important contribution to the available literature dealing with the parental loss of a child.

~From the Foreword by Julia Hinkle Penn, MD

Barbara Manger has written a moving, poetic story of a mother's efforts to come to terms with an unimaginable loss and the sorrow it brings. A "how to" book of the highest order, *Riding Through Grief* documents Manger's journey, in which she is upheld by her love for her son. The book offers a portrait of a family that although shaken by grief is also inspired by a son's joy in living, and ultimately finds a way to move forward.

~Jane Mandel, PhD, JD

I highly recommend *Riding Through Grief* for all seeking a path out of the throes of grief. Painfully honest, Barbara Manger spares us little as we experience the deep hurt in her heart. But we also share in the glimmers of hope and even happiness that gradually seep back into her life.

~Kathleen Huston Raab
Former City Librarian, Milwaukee, Wisconsin

Most of us do not talk freely about overwhelming grief. We find ourselves without the vocabulary necessary to adequately describe it and its powerful hold over us. Yet, in *Riding Through Grief*, Barbara Manger speaks out bravely about how her family found a way to not only respect the power of grief, but also begin life again. Barbara's book is a painting in prose that everyone should read.

~Janice Rhodes, JD

Riding Through Grief is a sorrowful yet joyful celebration of a young man's life. Having lost our daughter in a tragic accident, I know firsthand that Barbara tells it like it is. Her story is inspirational!

~Mardi James
Whitefish Bay, Wisconsin

Barbara Manger enjoys riding her bike on country roads, and riding with her twenty-nine- year-old son, Matt, was special. Sadly, her life changed forever as she faced the heartbreaking news that Matt had been struck down by an SUV while riding in a Chicago bike race. In the aftermath of this devastating time in Barbara's life, and amidst her grief and mourning, she has been remarkably creative and brave as she continues to face the challenges of daily life. And now, whether she is sad or happy, she still continues to ride her bike whenever she can. Barbara's story is one that will appeal to many people young and old.

~Lee Raffel, MSW, LCSW, LMFT
Author, *I Hate Conflict! Seven Steps to Resolving Differences with Anyone in Your Life*

RIDING THROUGH GRIEF

Barbara Manger

Point Comfort Press
Milwaukee, Wisconsin
www.RidingThroughGrief.com

Riding Through Grief by Barbara Manger
©2013 by Barbara Manger

Printed in the United States of America

17 16 15 14 13   1 2 3 4 5

ISBN: 978-0-9897923-1-8 (Paperback Edition)

Library of Congress Control Number: 2013947441

Cover photograph courtesy of Eric Oxendorf.
Bicycle illustration courtesy of Luke Manger-Lynch.

Excerpts from the funeral service in chapter 8 reprinted with permission of The Reverend Dr. Scott Stoner.

"Pueblo Blessing" in chapter 15 excerpted from *Prayers for Healing: 365 Blessings, Poems, & Meditations from Around the World* ©1997. Edited by Maggie Oman. Published by Red Wheel/Weiser, LLC (Newburyport, MA and San Francisco). www.redwheelweiser.com 800-423-7087. Reprinted with permission.

Editor: Priscilla Pardini
Developmental Editor: Kurt Chandler
Designer and Typographer: Kate Hawley
Production Coordinator: Susan Pittelman

This paper meets the requirements of ANSI/NISO.
The stocks used in the printing of this book are FSC certified.

Published by

Point Comfort Press
3318 North Lake Drive
Milwaukee, WI 53211
www.RidingThroughGrief.com

Oh, to love what is lovely, and will not last!
    What a task
      to ask

of anything, or anyone,

yet it is ours,
    and not by the century or the year, but by the hours.

    ~Mary Oliver, "Snow Geese"
    from *New and Selected Poems, Volume Two*

For my family and friends
who stepped in with their love.

Acknowledgments

WITH THANKS TO THOSE FAMILY MEMBERS AND FRIENDS WHO SHARED their memories of Matt, funny stories about him, and his sometimes quirky recipes.

With gratitude to Judy Bridges, who nudged me to begin, and to Kurt Chandler, who reviewed the original manuscript and offered insights and encouragement. With more thanks to Susan Pittelman, Priscilla Pardini, and Kate Hawley, whose skills brought this book to completion.

Foreword

It is often said that there is no greater loss than that of one's child. In my thirty-five years of experience as a clinical psychiatrist and as a former assistant professor of psychiatry at the Medical College of Wisconsin, I have encountered this truism over and over again when working with parents who have lost a child to an untimely death.

The insurmountable challenge for many of these individuals is just to find a way to go on. The loss they have experienced is usually highly personal and lonely, even when facing the post-death journey with other loved ones. At best, a parent who has lost a child is eventually able to function again, finding a way to once more experience life with all its joys, trials, and tribulations. Still, it is never the same life, and the parent is changed forever.

In *Riding Through Grief*, Barbara Manger recounts her traumatic experience of losing her beloved, younger son, Matt. An emotionally honest and bravely revealing story, it recalls moments of Matt's life that foreshadow his tragic cycling accident, as well as descriptions of the many tangible and intangible ways Barbara and her family sought to memorialize him. Writing with poignancy and a range of emotions, Barbara intimately describes the difficult journey that takes her from confronting an unbearable tragedy to finding a way to live a life forever changed. At the same time, her story serves as a loving, healing tribute to the spirit of the unique individual who was her son.

It is rare for a parent to completely "recover" from such an experience, and Barbara makes no such pretense. Yet, she has found a way to put one foot in front of the other and keep moving along the path of life.

Riding Through Grief offers hope and helpful insight to others trying to find their way through the loss of a loved one. It will be a valuable resource for family members and friends who accompany these individuals on their journeys, as well as for mental health and other health care professionals seeking more effective ways to help people experiencing such a loss. (The book's website, www.RidingThroughGrief.com, includes a very helpful set of questions designed to serve as a discussion guide for both formal and informal grief support groups.)

I highly recommend Barbara Manger's *Riding Through Grief*. It is an important contribution to the literature dealing with the loss of a child.

Julia Hinkle Penn, MD

Preface

THIS MEMOIR ABOUT THE LOSS OF MY SON MATT BEGAN AS AN ATTEMPT TO absorb the tragic and debilitating rupture of reality brought about by his sudden death. Although there was—and still is—no way to understand it, as I wrote I gradually became able to recognize and accept the new normal of life without him. I began to breathe into the life that is.

I have strained to recall the sweet, funny, and ordinary moments with Matt before they float beyond the reach of my mind's eye. Savoring these memories, I have found a profound gratitude for the twenty-nine years we shared, and take comfort in the fact that, as one friend told me, "You knew his whole life."

As I wrote over a period of three years, I began to think that reading about Matt and our family's painful struggle to live without him might be helpful to others. Perhaps it will offer perspective for those who have experienced debilitating loss. It might also provide insight and understanding for friends and acquaintances of those immersed in such struggles.

Although *Riding Through Grief* is a personal story, it deals with a distressingly common experience: the unexpected death of a loved one. In my search for solace, I often felt alone and lost. My deepest wish is that this book will help bring peace to others still trudging through the dark tunnel of grief.

Barbara Manger

CHAPTER 1

Riding on Country Roads

As I pedal west along Highway K in Kewaunee County in northeast Wisconsin, the autumn sun warms my back. The air is fresh but tinged with the sweet smell of recently fertilized fields. The remaining wildflowers—blue chicory, Queen Anne's lace, dried mullein stalks, masses of cadmium-tipped goldenrod, and delicate sprinklings of white aster—grace the roadside. Red willow, rusty sumac, and the yellow "butter-and-eggs" flowers growing low to the ground add soft accents. The blacktop ribbon I ride on unfurls in a straight line past rows of crisp cornstalks and dusty stubble—remnants of summer. The chirping of crickets and katydids rises and falls, interspersed with the high-pitched zing of locusts sounding out the season.

I watch for black and brown woolly bear caterpillars as they inch their way across what must seem to them a vast expanse of black asphalt. They cross the road this time of year, their routes perfectly perpendicular to the road's edge. This fall it appears that few have successfully maneuvered the trip. I avoid running over those still en route and others whose journeys have ended before they reached their destination. When I look up, beyond the rise in the distance I see the expanse of the blue-brown waters of Green Bay, the horizon of its west shore barely visible.

It is 2008, but I am remembering a similar day one year ago. "Come on, Mom," Matt had said, mounting his bike and inviting me to ride with him on the glorious backcountry roads we both love. "Biking in France has nothing over this," I said, as we rolled along. Small family farms, soft green and golden fields, cylindrical rolls of hay, the smell of earth and cows, and the occasional wave from a farmer on his tractor are pieces of this Wisconsin picture of pleasure.

Settled by Belgian farmers just before the turn of the twentieth century, this farmland at the base of the Door Peninsula of Wisconsin echoes the beauty of Flemish landscape painting. The names on mailboxes, barns, and road signs declare the early settlers' presence—Deterville, Mercier, Vandenhouten. We passed through the tiny villages of Champion, Thiry Daems, Frog Station, and larger Luxemburg, admiring the yard decorations popular in this region. Concrete boys and girls in wooden shoes, miniature windmills, gnomes, and pastel statues of the Virgin Mary enshrined in arched bathtubs decorate carefully mowed lawns surrounding lush flower and vegetable gardens.

We stopped for a minute on the roadside at a prosperous farm that, in addition to milk cows, raised veal. Wide-eyed calves housed in individual cages gazed at us as Matt said, "Mmmm," and I said, "Ick," just loud enough for him to hear. We laughed and rode on.

I remember admiring Matt on his bike, noting his height—six feet— and his young man's muscles as any mother or any woman would. He was at ease with his strength, and seemed unaware of his striking appearance. With his Roman nose, dark curly hair, and hands delicate for a man of his stature, he was indeed handsome. His deep brown eyes radiated energy and his zest for life. "How beautiful he is, how graceful," I thought.

Matt seemed happy to be riding with his mother, but I, of course, was slower than he. When he decided to burst ahead at his natural pace, he shouted back to me, "I'll wait for you at the stop sign." I pedaled with all my strength, laughing at this challenge, but could not keep up. He waited patiently at the stop sign, guzzling water. At last, I reached him, breathless and sweating.

"You're a good biker, Mom," he said with a big grin. I could think of nothing else I would rather be doing and nowhere I would rather be.

This fall I ride alone. When I squint, I can almost see Matt riding ahead of me. "Wait a minute, Matt," I want to shout. "I'll catch up to you." But I continue my ride solo, my thoughts focused on him.

As I return from the ride on exactly the roads we took together, a bird—a small owl, I think—swoops from a tree and crosses my path just at eye level. "Matt?" I ask aloud. My voice startles me. "Matt?" I ask again, as if he might be able to hear me. They *may* hear me—the owl and Matt. The owl disappears into a patch of woods and I brake, pull over onto gravel, and get off my bike for a better look. But he's gone.

Then, I remember. On the Sunday morning of Matt's fatal accident my husband, Bill Lynch, met Matt's wife, Elizabeth, and her father, Bob, at Matt and Elizabeth's home in Chicago. As they went down the front steps to the car to drive to the hospital to identify Matt, a huge owl flew directly across their path, silently flapping its wings.

Tears trickle down my cheeks as I gather myself together. I will not ride with Matt again, but I will ride with my memories of him.

CHAPTER 2

Bursting

MATT HAD A WAY OF DOING MOST EVERYTHING WITH A BURST—EVEN HIS birth. One minute I waddled and paced the shiny halls of the hospital, chatting with my kindly obstetrician. An hour later, there came Matt, with a burst and a cry. He was a beautiful baby, easy and sweet natured, born at 8:30 a.m., September 28, 1978, on my mother's birthday and two days after that of his three-year-old brother, Luke.

Other energy bursts pervade my memories. On a summer day when Matt was three, I gathered the boys up along with their cousins, eight-year-old Fritz and eleven-year-old Dylan. We piled into our old VW and headed north to Door County, the thumb-shaped peninsula of Wisconsin surrounded by Green Bay on the west and Lake Michigan on the east.

We planned an overnight stay at a one-room cabin built, but no longer owned by, my younger brother, Bob. We walked single file on a root-twined path through cedar woods to the tiny structure. Perched close to the Lake Michigan shore, the cabin has a high-pitched, shake-shingled roof above rustic, hand-hewn logs. It provides adequate shelter but no electricity or plumbing. We decided that trolls might live here when humans are absent.

I lay on my stomach on flat, sun-warmed limestone while the boys hopped from rock to rock, playing and splashing in the spray of icy waves. I watched their lively antics, listening to their shouts as they discovered crayfish and minnows. The day slid by as summer days do.

While I started a small campfire, the boys searched for long sticks. We slid the sticks into wieners and singed them over the fire. The burnt hot dogs in burnt buns were hot and juicy, flavored by the outdoors. S'mores, made with graham crackers, roasted marshmallows, and Hershey's chocolate bars, rounded out our meal. We stumbled in the fading light of dusk down to the lake to wash dishes, faces, and hands before bed. After climbing the ladder to the low-ceilinged loft, the boys wiggled, poked, and kicked until they nestled into spots of comfort, curling close together in the blackness. I read to them for nearly two hours, the mounds of sleeping bags a gentle rolling landscape in the flashlight's glow. As I read the last pages of *Pippi Longstocking*, their breathing quiet and even, a bat suddenly swooped over our heads—so close I could hear its fragile wings beating. The boys typically do not scream, but they did, and in unison—a high-pitched, piercing cry of fear. The bat dove again from the other direction, its silhouette illuminated, its magnified shadow speeding over us.

Matt bolted to his feet, still cocooned in his sleeping bag. Without warning, projectile vomit burst from his mouth, more than I thought his little belly could hold. My flashlight beamed on chunks of hot dog, marshmallow, and graham cracker, suspended in a cocoa-tinted liquid that flowed over the folds of our sleeping bags. Three boys groaned and buried their heads inside their bags. Matt looked stunned.

Squeezing the flashlight under my arm, I lugged bucket after bucket of water up the bumpy path from the lake, then climbed the ladder, again and again, to mop up the mess. The boys were no help. They continued to express their disgust at the smell of vomit and their alarm over the presence of the bat. "How many are there? How big are they?" they asked, maneuvering about to avoid the flowing review of our dinner. After the cleanup, I read for another hour to return tranquility to the pile of sleepy boys. Matt was the first to burrow back into his sleeping bag and nod off. I was the last. Likely the bat squeezed itself through a tiny crack into the safety of the outdoors to escape the flurry it created. We didn't see it again.

An essay I found between the pages of a blue spiral notebook reflected another burst of Matt's unbridled energy. Matt had embellished the notebook with his quirky, expressive doodles and sketches. The essay, a high school assignment, is a highly dramatized recollection of a childhood episode that apparently made a lasting impression.

"Big Wheel" by Matt Lynch, September 30, 1982

What? I can't watch TV for a week!" I barked with tears in my eyes. Whining and crying I stomped out of the door and slammed it with a crash. With all of my four-year-old strength, I opened the maroon garage door. I jumped onto my familiar red Dukes of Hazard big wheel and peeled out of my garage, dust shooting behind me. I looked down at the fuel gage, above the warning label that I had shredded off, half empty, the same as the sticker said when my parents bought it two years ago.

Cruising down the Summit Avenue sidewalk, all I could hear was the dull roar the wheels made and the clickity-clack of the cracks as I flew over them. Boss Hog, my parents, and the sheriff were no match for me. I just had to make it to the county line, out of all of their jurisdictions, like Bo and Luke did in the TV show. As I screeched around the turn onto Kenwood Boulevard, I knew I would never go home again.

When I reached the corner of Kenwood and Downer (about three blocks away), I was in foreign territory. The honking cars, people flying by on foot and bikes, and the flashing traffic lights were all new to me. I had no idea what to do. There was no way I could get across the street. The onslaught of traffic was too strong. The only thing I could do was stake out the position. I leaned over the hard plastic handlebars and started to cry. Bo and Luke, my childhood television idols, never got in a jam like this, and when they did, they just asked Uncle Jesse for help. . . .

I recall this incident clearly, with a smile, and from a slightly different viewpoint. My husband and I sent out a hastily gathered search party, an exuberant fleet of older neighborhood kids on bikes and Big Wheel tricycles, which scoured the neighborhood for the youngest of their group. While we did not think he would get very far on his plastic Big Wheel, we worried about the traffic in our urban neighborhood and about his thirst for adventure, even at four years old.

As Matt described later in his narrative, he was soon rescued: "What seemed like hours later, one of my neighbors, a boy about twelve years old, found me crying on the corner. . . . I made the long trek home and sat down to a PB and J sandwich."

Another example of Matt's boundless exuberance is described in a condolence letter I received from a beloved YMCA camp counselor relating his memories of Matt on a kayaking trip when he was twelve.

He was the smallest member of the group but the strongest and most determined paddler. His enthusiasm was contagious.

Midway into the trip, we were camping on Stockholm Island in the Apostle Islands in Lake Superior. Matt and several of the campers went down to the dock to fish and talk to the sail boaters. Observing a grill covered with enormous steaks hanging over the stern of a sailboat they asked if any food ever dropped over the side. The chef/captain replied that in twenty years never a crumb had gone overboard. Moments later the grill collapsed, plunging the steak into the icy depths of Lake Superior. Matt received consent from the steak owner that if he retrieved the steaks he could keep them. After several fruitless attempts at snagging the steaks, Matt selected the next logical choice—he dove in, swam down eight to ten feet and retrieved the steaks. That was the only trip I ever ate a steak dinner!

Next morning the sailboat captain and his wife delivered two dozen eggs, ham, steaks, and Rice Krispies treats to our campsite. An amazing trail event.

Years later, as a counselor at the same camp, Matt trained his ten-year-old campers to shout out his sentiment for the summer: "I'm alive, awake, alert, and enthusiastic!" It was a chant he'd exhort them to: "Repeat three times!"

I witnessed many impulsive acts during Matt's childhood. Most were innocent and harmless, humorous and high-spirited. In fourth grade, for example, he tossed butter pats, saved from lunch, hoping they would stick to the bathroom ceiling. He said his brother told him to do this. I choose to forget later bursts in high school and others during his college years that I didn't witness. A mother may never hear about all her son's escapades.

Luke told me that Matt and his buddies made late-night, cross-country ski trips through the streets of downtown St. Paul and Minneapolis during snowstorms in his four years at Macalester College in St. Paul. "I'm pretty sure that if he came across a busy road where the snow had been plowed or worn away by traffic, it didn't deter him from skiing through," said Luke. "I imagine those big, wet Minnesota flakes floating down and Matt cruising through the city."

Some of his bursts were more serious. One Saturday evening in January 1999, I answered the phone to hear, "Is this the Lynch residence?" The voice, calling from a hospital in Redwing, Minnesota, announced that Matt had injured his head snowboarding. Treating the injury was beyond the hospital's capacity, so they transferred him to the Mayo Clinic. In a panic, Bill and I grabbed a change of clothes and flew to Rochester, Minnesota. At the Mayo Clinic a doctor informed us that Matt had a concussion but no other serious injuries and that he would be all right in a few days. In a darkened room, I saw Matt, his full six feet filling the length of the hospital bed, his dark hair against the white pillow. His eyes were closed, an IV drip in his arm. As I sat beside the bed, I noticed his hairy toes protruding past the end of the sheet. "This is my child," I thought. "He has become a man."

Other accidents flash to mind. Once in his sixth summer Matt came running to me, screaming with pain after falling off his bike into a nest of ground bees. When he reached me the bees were still stinging him on his arms, legs, and through the seat of his shorts. I recall his tender little buttocks swelling with welts as I rubbed on soothing ointment. How could I have prevented this? When he was eight, he slipped on the high dive after swimming class and fell to the tile below. He needed close attention afterward, but did not suffer a concussion or other injuries. If I had been at the lesson would I have said, "Don't go on the high dive," "Watch out, it's too high," or "Don't fall"?

I do not believe I could have prevented these accidents any more than I could have protected him from the snowboarding incident. Although Bill and I did not encourage recklessness in our sons, we did not discourage adventures or hold them back from exploring the world in energetic ways. When they were children we feared for their safety and protected them to the extent that we were able. In their adulthood that impulse did not change, but our reach and influence as parents could not restrain them.

I wish I could say that while Bill and I sat awkwardly in the hospital chairs in the dark, greenish light we had a deep and meaningful conversation with Matt about danger, risk taking, and our love and concern for him—but that did not happen. When he opened his eyes he was groggy and surprised to see us. "I'm out of here," he said, seeing no need to remain in the hospital. Because of what I took to be intense embarrassment, Matt would not talk about the accident nor did he appear to listen to us. Was facing his own vulnerability too difficult? Was the reality of his risk taking too frightening to confront?

After his funeral, Matt's friends wrote of escapades and outings with Matt—those that could be shared with a grieving mother. David, a friend since the age of three, wrote a lengthy letter recounting many memories of Matt. Among them: Matt's "explosives" stage, when he made "works" bombs out of drain cleaner and aluminum foil, and terrorized the neighborhood's jack-o'-lanterns. "One day 'works' bombs were no longer exciting and Matt decided to move on to gasoline-based explosives," David wrote. "I reluctantly joined him as we detonated a primitive Molotov cocktail in Lake Park and were subsequently interrogated and released by a park worker."

Of course, Luke shared many bursts with Matt.

> One of my last nights out with Matt was in Chicago in 2007 on Thanksgiving weekend. We went to a couple of blues clubs. Matt and I were packed into the back of a club ordering drinks at the bar. The guy next to me had a cigarette, which was wafting smoke right into my face while his back was turned. Matt told me how great the smoking ban was going to be—it would go into effect in

a month. This guy's cigarette was really bothering me. I told Matt how I was going to flick it out of his hand. Matt watched incredulously as I turned my back, kept my eye on the cigarette and quickly jerked it out of the guy's hand, sending it to the ground without the guy realizing who had done it. A couple of bars and drinks later, Matt gave this silly game a shot, but with a six-feet-five, barrel-chested Italian. We were lucky to get out of the bar unscathed, and a table or two overturned as we fled. Running down the block, we figured at least our lungs were fresher!

When Matt entered a room, it was with a burst of sunshiny energy. He filled any space with it. I do not think he was aware of the effect of his presence. Nor would he know the effect of his absence.

The thought is chilling, but perhaps the way that Matt died was fitting. He burst forth into a Chicago intersection on his bike. He was hit. He left his earthly body instantly. No lingering. No suffering. No painful goodbyes. Had Matt been offered the unlikely responsibility of choosing how he would exit this world, he might have chosen to do so this very way. He would not, however, have chosen that particular time.

He was riding in a local Chicago Sunday morning race series. His fellow riders reported that Matt was out at the front of the group among the leaders, riding side by side with his teammate Nico when he began to sprint ahead. Matt sped into the complicated intersection where West Irving Park Road connects with North Damen and North Lincoln Avenues, likely not seeing the red light. An SUV entered the intersection and struck Matt, hurling him to the pavement. His fellow riders quickly realized that their efforts to revive him would not succeed. Nor would those of the rescue squad, which arrived immediately. Nico held Matt.

A few days later on the blog site created for Matt, Nico wrote, "Matt and I joked about how our road bikes were almost identical. I took advantage of the many times throughout these last few rides where I found myself tucked behind him trying to rest and make sense of the world from within his draft. I will miss this luxury. How much effect we have on each other."

Perhaps I did not have the proper effect on my sons. Did I caution them enough about the dangers that could be lurking anywhere? I remember giving all the standard motherly warnings: "Hold my hand. Chew your food slowly. Do not run with a lollipop in your mouth. Hold a pair of scissors point down. Do not talk to strangers. Look both ways when you cross a street. Wear a life jacket. Check the rear view mirror."

Like every mother, I worried about my children and their welfare. As Luke and Matt grew to adulthood, my worrying decreased but never ceased. I still had concerns about their safety. But I did not worry about them dying, and never considered that Matt might die before me or that he would die young, like this.

In just an instant, in a burst of energy crossing an intersection, Matt was no longer alive, no longer of this world. I cried and cried, "Why couldn't it have been me?" I gladly would have given my life so that he could continue his, but this thought has no link to reality. The reality is, in any one disastrous, random moment, life can change or end. There is no protection against this.

I have often wondered about what may or may not be attributable to the randomness of life. I suppose meeting Bill was a random event, but that we married, had children, and have survived as a couple was not.

In 1969, Bill and I met in North Carolina where I held my first teaching position in the art department at Fayetteville State University. During my second, challenging year at this historically black university, Bill was stationed at nearby Fort Bragg and had just applied for release from the army as a conscientious objector. A first lieutenant in a military intelligence unit, he had completed law school at the University of Chicago and worked briefly at a large law firm in Providence, Rhode Island, before entering the army to fulfill his ROTC commitment.

War and violence are not in Bill's nature. In his spare time while he waited to hear the results of his application, he counseled young GIs, possible conscientious objectors, at the Quaker Meeting House in Fayetteville. After a considerable wait, he was granted a discharge as a conscientious objector. Apparently, the Army considered that the better position for Bill (and the army) was outside its ranks.

We married six months after meeting, and became acquainted during our forty years of marriage. I am grateful to Bill for convincing me to be a mother, a role I never thought I would fill. I had envisioned myself moving to New York City and living as an artist. I have had a career as an artist and teacher, but the experience of giving birth to and raising two sons has been more meaningful and life changing than I could have imagined. I cherish the many powerful, painful, and sweet moments of our lives with them.

CHAPTER 3

Early Cooking

THE WINTER SUN HAS SET AS I WALK UP THE BACK STEPS INTO THE KITCHEN, weighed down by grocery bags and books. As I enter the kitchen, an acrid, smoky smell greets me. Our blond, male babysitter sits hunched over his homework, oblivious to my arrival and unaware of the culinary chaos around him. Matt, a fifth grader, is grinning at me, bits of yellow stuff stuck to his smooth, rosy cheeks and in his curly hair. He stands between the oven and the sink, waving a welcome with a big wooden spoon. As I step closer, sugar grinds underfoot as I sidestep to avoid a pool of congealed goo.

"What is this?" I ask. I cannot help but smile at Matt and his sweetness, but I also feel the need to maintain my role as detective and disciplinarian.

Pans and utensils hide the countertops, and over the edge of one slides a glob of gelatinous, yellow stuff. Water from the faucet splashes down on bowls and measuring cups and the cracked eggshells scattered among them. An empty milk carton lies sideways on the floor. Most of the cupboards are open, their contents in disarray. With a sweeping flair, Matt opens the oven to reveal a brown, mushroom-shaped form billowing from a round pan.

With great care he removes the swelling blob from the oven and plops it on the counter. It sighs and deflates. "Mmm *hmm,*" he says. "I think I got it this time." The sitter turns, blinking at this organism and at Matt. "What is it?" he asks.

"Mmm *hmm,*" Matt says again. "A German pancake. Try it." The sitter shakes his head but I stick a spoon into the mass, blow, and bravely try a hot mouthful. An amazing concoction it is: spongy, slippery, sweet, and grainy—unlike a German pancake or any other food I've ever tried. Although not unpleasant, one bite is sufficient. I notice that Matt does not taste his latest effort but does appear content with its outcome. The sitter hefts his backpack and leaves, forgetting about his pay, and I turn to the dishes. I would like to remember that we merrily cleaned the kitchen together, but I do not think that happened.

An earlier cooking event had come about spontaneously when we visited my aunt at the Oregon seashore. Other than cookie baking under my supervision, this was probably Luke and Matt's first adventuresome cooking partnership—a spirited, sometimes crazy culinary collaboration they continued throughout Matt's lifetime. Matt was five, and Luke, eight. In the mist at low tide they climbed the craggy rock ledges along the shore and discovered that the little pools and crannies were teeming with life— strange creatures unknown to us midwesterners. Bill, raised on the East Coast, was able to recognize some as limpets, mussels, and barnacles, but others were foreign to him, too.

The boys gathered these clinging, shelled critters, prying them off rocks and dropping them into a grocery bag. I cannot now imagine that I thought this was all right, but they carried them to the cottage and, to the horror of my aunt, boiled the creatures and ate them with gusto and lemon juice, smiling as they picked and pulled the coiled flesh from their shells.

Matt first learned the discipline and art of cooking from Brahim Hadj-Moussa, known as "Hadj," or "Boss," to his employees. A native Algerian, Hadj is the chef and owner of the Barbary Fig restaurant where Matt worked while a student at Macalester College in St. Paul, Minnesota. Nestled in a charming Victorian house for more than twenty-five years, the Barbary Fig is rated one of the best restaurants in the Twin Cities. The menu radiates Hadj's roots in North Africa and time he spent in Provence, France. He skillfully combines the flavors of cinnamon, thyme, cumin, coriander, garlic, ginger, and mint to enhance slow-simmered *tagines*—stews of lamb, rabbit, and chicken accompanied by chutneys and couscous.

Hadj is ruggedly handsome, swarthy, and animated, a caring man loved and respected by the college students who work for him and a mentor to Matt. Under Hadj's wing, Matt developed a passion for cooking that became a way for him to direct his creativity and nearly unlimited energy. He strove to meet Boss's exacting standards and emulated his style. Hadj recognized his role and gave Matt his guidance and advice. After Matt left for New York City, he and Hadj talked often on the phone.

"He only worked for me a few months, but it seemed like I knew Mateo for a long time," Hadj told me, using the name he had given Matt. "I knew I would be talking to him until the day I died. It's too bad. I wish it wasn't like this. You have no idea what's going to happen. That is the nature of life. I told him to play and work until he had more experience for opening a business. Wait until you are forty. Learn a lot. Until then, work as a chef, work as a sous chef."

Hadj enjoyed Matt's company. "Mateo was always fun and funny. Monday nights were the slow nights of the week. I hired waitresses who might be problems on busier nights," he said, laughing. Hadj remembered that Matt called these two waitresses "Dumb" and "Dumber."

He also recalled Matt's dedication.

> From the beginning, I saw the passion he had. I tapped into that. I told him to go for it. . . .
>
> You have no idea what is coming next. The last discussion I had with him, it was the Monday before the Sunday of the accident. He had started to do curing of meat and ham. He was so focused on charcuterie. It was going to be new in the US. I told him it was great to have this idea. But don't start a business right now. In your twenties is too soon to start. You have a whole life ahead of you. Don't rush. Play as much as you can, then come talk to me.
>
> But Sunday came and everything went in the sky.

Matt's studies in anthropology took a back seat to cooking, but his major professor was supportive of Matt's culinary interests. For the final project in his senior seminar on Mongolian Anthropology, Matt put on a Mongolian wedding feast for the class, cooked and served in the basement of a dormitory. At home, Bill and I laughed at his quirky request: "Dad, can I have a little extra money to buy a goat?" How could he say no? Matt searched throughout Minneapolis and Saint Paul, eventually locating a Muslim market selling whole, butchered goats. We chuckled again when he described the Somali shop owner's insistence that Matt bargain over the price before he would sell the creature.

Matt followed Mongolian custom by gathering male and female rocks—their gender determined by their location on the banks of the Mississippi River. He tossed these into the pot to boil with the goat, vegetables, and vegetable stock, then served the dish with traditional dumplings. Matt told us that Jack Weatherford, his professor and a well-known expert on Mongolia, said it was the best *khorkhog* he had ever eaten. The wedding feast was a success and earned Matt an A.

CHAPTER 4

New York City

AT AGE TWENTY-THREE, A FEW DAYS BEFORE SEPTEMBER 11, 2001, MATT moved to New York City for an internship at the French restaurant La Grenouille in Midtown Manhattan, about four miles north of the World Trade Center. He stayed with friends in Brooklyn, where, from the roof of their building they watched the second World Trade Center tower collapse. As Luke, Bill, and I watched the same sad sight on TV, a phone call from Matt's friend Masami in Minneapolis let us know that Matt was all right. She remembered that just before their call was cut short, Matt said, "Planes are falling out of the sky." Masami thoughtfully forwarded to us the e-mail she had sent to Matt at 2:22:57 that afternoon.

> Mateo! I called you earlier and I got disconnected like ten seconds after you picked up! I'm glad you picked up your phone, though, cuz I feel better knowing you aren't hurt. I told Aaron I got a hold of you for like five seconds and he had enough foresight to call your mom and let her know that you had picked up the phone. She's worried,

21

though. Take care of yourself. Be safe. Call me when you can. I'll keep trying your cell.

Love, Masami

And, on the following day at 11:40 a.m., we were relieved and happy to hear from Matt.

NY is the strangest place now. Smoke continues to billow from the southern third of Manhattan, which is entirely closed to people. There are two aircraft carriers and a battleship that I could see from the roof this morning, circling. Everybody knows somebody who is either dead, injured, or missing. They're talking 20,000 dead on the news. Tomorrow 6,000 army special engineer troops arrive in Manhattan, armed.

On the way to work today, the train was full because few are running, and from Brooklyn to Union Square, about six stops, the train rolled on. Not a word was said by anyone on board, but when the train passed through empty, deserted platforms covered with a thick layer of ash: Bowling Green, Fulton Street, Brooklyn Bridge, Wall Street, Canal Street, Lafayette, people silently hung their heads. When I got out in Midtown at 51st Street, there was nobody about. A few lone cabs on the street, no noise, no honking, few pedestrians—a ghost town. It was eerie, scary, quiet. I didn't even bother looking down the streets when crossing Park Avenue and Madison Avenue. No cars on the road.

People at work began their day wandering around saying empty hellos with glazed looks on their faces. A number of my co-workers had family members who had been killed the day before. As the day continued, people picked up their heads a little bit. Being in a place with no windows, no contact with the outside, and hard work made most ignore what was going on. When the night was dragging on, this isolation was ended by thick smoke drifting into the building from outside when the wind shifted. Oh well. Back to work tomorrow. I'd rather toil than watch the news.

One of Matt's first tasks at this posh restaurant was making sandwiches for the rescue workers—quite a switch from the usual French fare. Soon the restaurant was open and back on schedule.

Since early childhood, Matt demonstrated the ability to focus completely—mentally and physically—on whatever drew his interest. When he played his saxophone as a preteen and teenager his attention could not be drawn away. Listening to music was a total body experience. He would say, "Listen, listen, listen, to this," and shut his eyes as his head bobbed with the rhythm, feeling it with muscle, fiber, bone. This ability to focus so intently served him well as he applied himself to the tasks of cooking. He rose to the demands of the hard, physical labor and accepted the kitchen hierarchy and the quirks and demands of the chef. The friendly, hard-working Dominicans who did the prep and cleanup work gained his admiration, and he delighted in practicing his Spanish or having a beer with them.

Matt loved everything about working in a kitchen—even the heat. He especially loved the results. I watched from afar with pride as he grew and matured in this position, meeting with courage, wisdom, and his keen sense of humor the challenge of work in a famous kitchen and the difficulty of living in Manhattan at this terrible time.

CHAPTER 5

Lunch at La Grenouille

IN MARCH 2002, THREE FRIENDS AND I—MIDDLE-AGED, BUNDLED-UP women with packages—squeeze into a taxi. We are laughing and exhilarated as we make our way from museums and shopping to prestigious La Grenouille, the classic French restaurant located for forty-five years in a quaint, two-story building at Three East Fifty-Second Street in the heart of Midtown Manhattan. A massive bouquet of bright, yellow forsythia blooms in stately welcome in a large window just above the discreet entryway.

A review in the dining guide *Zagat* quoting La Grenouille patrons describes the restaurant as: "The epitome of 'everlasting elegance,'" . . . and "'top-of-the-line' all the way, catering to a glamorous 'money crowd (real jewelry)' with 'extraordinary food and service' and 'dazzling flowers.'" Notes *Zagat*, "steep prices . . . are a given."

Giggling in anticipation of what awaits us, we step in from the damp spring day. The dignified maître d' greets us with the proper balance of cordiality and propriety. We wind our way among the tables into the restaurant's warm, subdued atmosphere. Gold damask-covered walls, soft

25

lighting, and gleaming silver and crystal whisper that refinement and opulence abide here.

Once settled at our table we admire the lustrous, white Royal Worcester china and weighty, white napery. The French waiter in a smart tuxedo gracefully pours complimentary glasses of champagne.

"You are wishing to see Matt?" he asks. "Which one of the ladies is the mother?"

Just then Matt strides out from the kitchen in his white toque and spotless cook's jacket. He exudes energy, and all around him swirl tantalizing smells and the warmth of the kitchen. I beam.

"Hi, Mom. Hi, everybody." No hug or kiss; he's working. He makes suggestions from the menu. "If you like sweetbreads that might be a good choice—these are veal—braised, with a delicate, creamy flavor." I search my mind for what sweetbreads are and vaguely remember that they are thymus glands. I return to the menu.

Matt asks, "Do you have any food allergies? Any special requests?" I say nothing but am certain I am allergic to thymus gland. He says he hopes that we will enjoy our lunch, then heads back to the kitchen. I am bursting with pride for this sweet, exuberant young man, thrilled that my friends are getting to see him in his recently discovered profession.

The elegant waiter poises—pen over pad—as we select, then change, our choices, and then change them again. He smiles patiently. "You may take your time, ladies. We have the whole day," he says with sincerity.

We chat, look around for celebrities and "real jewelry," and drink more champagne, imagining what will be set before us. When the plates are wheeled in on a little serving cart, the three waiters lift the silver domes with flourish and we inhale the sight, the steam, and the smells. Then we begin. Each forkful is heavenly, each a mouthful to close your eyes and sigh for. Green herb sprigs—dill, thyme, rosemary—artfully perch on plate rims. Twisted, paper-thin lemon slices with sole, a tiny wedge of pate, and unidentifiable bits of this or that nearly cause me to slip from my chair to the floor with pleasure. This is not nouveau or fusion food, but proper, classic French cuisine.

Partway into our meal Matt again appears at our table, flushed from the heat and the pace in the kitchen. We "ooh." We "aah." That's all he needs to hear. The waiters dote on us, pouring more champagne than anyone should drink on a Saturday afternoon. A distinguished, silver-haired waiter glides over to our table and, in an exquisite French accent, compliments Matt. "You are the mother of Matt? He is a kind young man, so friendly. He shows much talent as a cook," he says. "He shows the promise we look for." I beam again.

Three hours later, another waiter, with a slight smile, asks, "Would you like your coffee now or with your second dessert?" After the mousse and tiny pastries, a silver plate of dainty chocolate truffles appears before us, then coffee. When nearly every bit of goodness has vanished, Charles Masson Jr., the sophisticated, gracious, and second-generation owner, comes to our table and—with a distinguished bow—offers us each a pink gift bag holding a copy of his book on flower arranging, illustrated with his own delicate watercolors.

The gentle clink of china, murmuring voices, and soft lighting lull us into quiet. We sink into this moment of satisfaction until Matt emerges, beads of sweat on his forehead, radiating energy, to ask how everything was. "Perfect" is the only answer. However, it is not only the perfection of the meal and its ambience that I experience. It is also my love for and pride in my son—now a young man—and my joy in knowing that he has discovered creative work he loves and that he delights in sharing with others. I am perfectly content.

On another visit to New York, on a cold and windy day, Matt leads Bill and me on a different culinary adventure—a perfect contrast to La Grenouille. Two subways and a numbingly frozen walk at his quick-paced stride take us to a tiny falafel place in the West Village. "You are going to love this!" he says as we press against a crowd of other customers into a steamy, garlicky, closet-sized space. We order and then squeeze onto stools at the counter, coat sleeves rubbing and noses running and only a foot away from the cookstove. In a minute or two the grizzled-haired cook slams our plates across the counter, bouncing the Pita bread and falafel balls and almost shimmying the lettuce, tomato, and yogurt sauce off the plates. In heavy coats, flushed and sweating, we down generous heaps of this greasy, spicy fare. Not my favorite, but I delight in Matt's zeal and his openness to all possibilities as he shows his midwestern parents this hole-in-the-wall and its no frills, no fanfare food.

Both our sons followed Bill's adventuresome eating preferences. If turtle mole appeared on the menu, he ordered it, and the boys followed suit or one-upped him. When the boys were in their early teens the three of them waged hot pepper-eating contests, eating raw the most flamingly hot ones while making great efforts to appear nonchalant even as sweat beaded on their foreheads. After reaching legal age, they sought out the bars and restaurants that served the best chicken wings and discussed their features and flavors. Tiring of this, they searched for the best fried cheese curds. The geographic range for these was limited as this gooey, greasy specialty is unique to Wisconsin.

Perhaps the boys' earliest adventuresome food experiences were with my father, whom they called "Buppy." Once, when their chins just reached tabletop height, he invited us and other friends to an elegant Christmas Eve seafood buffet. Following their grandfather's example they tipped back their heads to slurp oysters from their shells, allowing the slimy globs to slide down their little throats. They took full advantage of the buffet, amazing everyone by consuming adult-sized portions. To our amusement and to the delight of his grandfather, Matt, the youngest in our party, stuffed himself. After raw oysters, he progressed to oyster stew and then to other seafood dishes, bypassing the salads and vegetables for seconds and thirds of tiny cream puffs, cheesecake, chocolate-covered strawberries, and Christmas cookies. Like a boa constrictor, he barely ate for several days afterward. At an early age Matt gave not a thought to how food was prepared, but simply enjoyed it with gusto and a grin.

CHAPTER 6

Finding Out

EACH OF US IN MATT'S IMMEDIATE FAMILY HEARD THE TERRIBLE NEWS IN different parts of the country. Of course, Elizabeth, Matt's wife, who lived in Chicago, was the first to find out.

On February 24, 2008, Sunday, I got up as usual but I was alone because Matt had left early for a bicycle race. . . .

He had slept in the guest room the night before so that his alarm would not wake me when he wanted to get up: five o'clock. At ten I took a bath and was disrupted because the phone kept ringing. I thought it odd because it was Sunday and also, no one ever called on that line. So I got out of the bath and answered it. It was a woman from the hospital and she said could I come down as soon as possible? I immediately got worried and said, "Oh God! Matt. What did he do now? Did he break a leg or something?" No, she couldn't explain, but could I please come down right away. So I got dressed and drove the quick ten minutes to the hospital. It was a sunny, cold February morning.

I walked into a group of people—Matt's fellow riders— in the waiting room. They stared at me as I strode in. I felt the energy in the room and my heart began to sink. I knew, but I didn't know. Didn't want to know. When the hospital staff told me to wait for the social worker to talk to me, then I knew what had happened. I knew he was dead. Why else would a social worker need to talk to me? They brought me into a small room with bright lights, a table, a chair, and a telephone. Everything happened really fast and I don't remember the words, but I remember asking the plump social worker, "He's dead, right?" She nodded. It was a blur from there. I called my mom. I was asked to call Matt's parents, which I did not want to do, but I did not want them finding out from anyone else. I called Bill. I called Luke. It was the most awful feeling to be the bearer of such news. I did not cry though. Not yet. After I made all the calls, I said I wanted to go home. A policewoman put her arms around my shoulders and walked me out of the hospital. It was twenty-six degrees but I did not feel cold. I did not feel anything. I said, "There's no way I can drive myself home." So she drove me and my car to my house and stayed with me for a while.

Soon my parents arrived. I cried the hardest when my father hugged me. He felt strong and warm and I just let go. Later, I decided not to go to the hospital to see his body, but my mom and Bill did. Sometimes I wish I had, but sometimes not. In the evening, my dad, my dog, and I took a walk. Just as we stepped outside, a huge owl swooped in front of us and perched in the tree across the street. It was dusk, but yet I could see it most definitely was a barn owl. We looked at each other for a good minute and then it flew off. It was a strange moment of respite from the intensity of the day: a large owl, in the middle of downtown Chicago. Looking back, besides the obvious, the worst and most difficult moment was calling Matt's family. At that point in my life (and even now, years later), having to tell his family was the single most difficult thing I have ever had to do.

About the same time that Sunday, I was sitting on a round *zafu* cushion in an early-morning meditation session on the first day of a yoga-training workshop in Houston. I was ill at ease, wiggling, not relaxing, working too hard to focus my thoughts. I was worrying about my phone, which was in my bag out of reach behind me. I had not turned it off and the thought that it might ring and shatter the silence was causing me anxiety. My thoughts were stuck on the phone. I was tense, waiting for the sound. At last, when the leader signaled an end to the half-hour session, I lunged to shut it off.

At the break I hurried to my room for breakfast, where my phone did ring, bringing Bill's strained voice and words of horror. I crumpled to my knees. "He was my baby," was all I could say. I got into the shower. Wash it away. Wash it away with needles of hot water.

Wrapped in a towel, dripping with water and tears, I answered a knock at the door. Lex, the yoga and meditation teacher, reached out to hug me. "I just can't imagine," Lex said. I heard this comment again and again from others. "Don't even try," became my standard answer. Behind him, a maid who was vacuuming in the motel corridor dropped her vacuum cleaner and came to put her arms around me. This was the start of unexpected but welcome demonstrations of caring from friends and strangers alike.

Luke and his wife, Kathy, arrived to accompany me from Houston to Milwaukee, a journey I could not have made alone. They held me in their loving care and together we cried. Bill was standing alone waiting for us in Milwaukee. I do not remember much about the trip, the arrival, and the return to our house.

Earlier that morning, a sunny Wisconsin winter day, Bill had been heading to an area west of Milwaukee to cross-country ski. He was feeling a happy glow from his surprise leap year birthday party a few days before, reflecting on the toasts and good wishes. Just before entering the westbound freeway, he pulled the car over to answer a call from Elizabeth. She said, "Bill, I have really bad news. Matt was hit. Matt didn't make it." She was calling from a hospital in Chicago.

"What are they doing for him?" asked Bill. With intense anguish, she said again, "Bill, he didn't make it." "No," Bill said, over and over.

"I couldn't accept this," he told me later. Elizabeth told him there was nothing to do. Her parents were on their way to Chicago. Bill drove home. He called Luke. He called me. He drove to the hospital in Chicago. He went in to see Matt. "I'm glad I did this," he said. "It made Matt's death immediately real." He drove back to Milwaukee. "It was a long day," he said.

Recalled Luke, "I was at my house in Wyoming scrambling around, packing up fishing gear and business clothes, and getting ready to drive to Cheyenne, planning to stop on the way to fish, then spend a couple days in meetings and legislative hearings. My phone kept ringing and I ignored it for a while. Finally I realized there were several calls, and I got a bad feeling. I spoke to Elizabeth, who told me what happened. It was not believable."

CHAPTER 7

Prelude to the Service

I SCARCELY REMEMBER THE DAYS AFTER THE ACCIDENT. BUT I DO remember the numbness, the crying, the disbelief, the inability to sleep. One clear memory is of Bill: stalwart, shouldering his role as the strong one. How did he do this? How was he able to hold himself and us together? From an early age Bill was the reliable and responsible one in his birth family, and he held that role in our family as well. Unwavering, steady, and strong, he was the one we depended on in any situation. He cried, he wept. But he understood that we needed him to ground us, so he did.

In the kitchen one of those first few days, staring at the orange teakettle Matt had given me, I heard the backdoor rattle open, then shut. Stomping boots released snow on the doormat, then Bill stepped into view. "I'm home," he called, his usual evening greeting. His cheekbones, protruding below the rim of his knit cap, glowed pink from walking our dog. He half smiled. For an instant I thought he was going to tell me there had been a mistake, that Matt was fine. I thought for a deluded instant that everything might be normal again.

I remember going to the funeral home and making plans with Rev. Scott Stoner, the wise and soulful man who five years earlier had married Matt and Elizabeth. He would now conduct the funeral service. We sat where efforts to create a "living" room were evident. The pale blue-and-silver chairs were selected, I am certain, for their subdued colors, but I found them irritating in their blandness: satiny, slippery, and formal. A black statue of Cupid balanced on tiptoe in one corner, his bow playfully raised. On each end of the mantle, porcelain vases held carefully arranged, dusty silk flowers. The scent of artificial floral air freshener hung in the air. I assume it was necessary in this place where death is stored. There was no way to find comfort here.

Matt's beautiful widow sat stiffly, her parents, brother, and sister bolstering her. Luke, Bill and I, Scott, and the funeral director completed the circle. We saw too clearly each other's red eyes, distorted faces, and hunched shoulders.

"Do you know the wishes of the deceased?" I heard the unctuous funeral director ask. "The deceased"? Matt had many wishes for his life, but I did not know what they were on this matter. I do not think he had any. At the age of four he wished for a remote control butterfly for his birthday. At age fifteen, he wished he were sixteen so he could get his driver's license. At twenty-nine, he and his wife wished for a child. He wanted to start a business, snowboard with his brother, travel to Spain with his friend Nick.

This haunting question—"Do you know the wishes of the deceased?"—trails me like a cyclist's orange caution flag.

Of course, at age twenty-nine, Matt—the deceased—had not made any plans for a funeral, and how could we? Scott saved us with sensitive suggestions and the appropriate questions. "Who would like to speak?"

he asked softly. "What music did Matt like?" With his nudging and gentle guidance, we discussed what would be the main message of this event. Bill, barely audible, said, "I want to speak." Luke lifted his hand slightly then dropped it saying, "I will too." Gray-faced Elizabeth said with firm resolve, "I am going to say something." I said defiantly, though barely able to speak, "I am not coming." To show up here in this place harboring death was bad enough. Knowing his remains were in the next room, I still couldn't imagine that his life had ended. A ceremony to recognize this was beyond my coping abilities. If I did not attend I would not have to recognize that his death was a reality. I could attempt to put it away, ignore the sheer horror of losing my baby boy.

We sat immobile for several moments, painful silence upon us, until the solicitous funeral director, hovering, nodding, and bobbing in a cloud of aftershave, leaned over my shoulder. In a stage whisper, his lips close to my ear, he asked, "Do you want to view Matt?"

"View him?" I asked. I had not really thought about this possibility.

As I hesitated, Luke, several chairs away, shook his head. "No, Mom, don't." And so I declined the last chance I would have to see my handsome son. Was he wearing his biking clothes? Was he lying on—what would it be—a stainless steel cart? A gurney? In the slide-out drawer of a cooler? Not for a second have I regretted this decision. Luke had "viewed" him and Bill had seen Matt in the hospital in Chicago. Bill said, "Matt just wasn't there anymore." He said he had left his body, instantly. I can imagine this and it is enough. I choose to hold in my mind's eye images of his liveliness and his great energy and vitality during his life here.

At a gathering the evening before the service I stood among family and friends. I was astonished. They were dealing with Matt's death by laughing, drinking, eating. They were coping by bringing his stories and jokes, his very presence, into this setting. They were feeling him here with us. Matt had loved all these people: his brother, Luke; his childhood friends David and Micah; his cousins, Dylan and Fritz; his college friends Nick, Andrea, Aaron, and Masami; and his Uncle Bob and Aunt Betsy. They appeared to hover closer to each other than usual, likely for comfort, but I also considered that perhaps they were creating a barrier to protect me from what might be my self-inflicted death or death from grief. I saw them as though behind a rain-spattered window, their talking and laughter muffled and far from me. From this distance I decided I would, after all, attend the service and that I would speak. How could I miss what I thought would be my last chance to convey to others—to Matt's friends, to our family's friends—who Matt had been in our lives? I had been the first to hold him and speak to him after his birth. I wanted to be among the last to speak in his memory. I couldn't *not* do it, but to compose myself enough to stand in front of others and speak of my beautiful, lost son seemed beyond the realm of possibility.

Early the following morning, February 28, 2008, I pulled on a wool hat, boots, and a favorite old jacket and walked along icy sidewalks to the park near our house. Following the walkway that diagonally crosses the park, I passed the warming house and the abandoned ice rink where our family skated when the boys were young. I crossed the footbridge guarded by stone lions wearing seasonal snow crowns. For several years, in all seasons, I pushed a stroller over this bridge. Later I traded it for a bicycle to ride beside two small boys.

Across the bridge, on the south side of the ravine, I found an ice-crusted park bench where I sat and leaned back, staring up at branches creating inky calligraphy against a silver sky. I heard no birds, no footsteps on this frigid day—only the occasional eerie creak of a frozen branch. I clenched and unclenched my hands inside my mittens, and mumbling to myself, began to consider what I could say. After what might have been half an hour of shivering and muttering, I had convinced myself that I could perform this daunting task, could carry out my duty as bereaved mother. Speaking aloud, coaching myself in a raspy voice, I said, "Barbara, you can do this. You have to do this. You can do it for Matt." Then rising from my icy seat I noticed a small plaque on the backrest of the bench engraved with a quotation from Anton Chekhov that read: "We will learn to appreciate there will be times when the trees will be bare . . ."

What day could feel more barren than this? How dead the world, the park, the black strokes of branches tapering to nothing.

I hurried home, resolved to do my part in the service. The gate to our backyard scraped against crusty snow when I shoved it to enter. I lay down, flat on my back in the yard under the graceful maple, sinking into the snow as our boys had once done to make snow angels here. When the cold seeped through my jacket I was forced to get up and go inside to dress for the service.

I dug out the blue funeral suit from the back of the closet and noticed a scarf that Matt and Elizabeth had bought me in Paris when he attended Le Cordon Bleu. They had said it looked like something I would wear: long and shocking pink, with spritely little yellow-and-blue threads sticking out and wildly animating the surface of the fabric. I had to wear it. A treasured friend, standing by to answer doors and phones and keep our household in order, helped me tie several knots to rein in its vitality. At the edge of my vision I could see the pink cloud and the little springy strings floating—a brilliant flash of color on the darkest day of my life.

"That scarf is really you," remarked several people on that dreadful morning. Had they known my heart and mind that day they would not have said this. *Really me?* I felt as dead as Matt. For over a month I avoided looking into mirrors. I turned my head when I passed one. I looked down into the sink when I brushed my teeth. If I could not see myself, if I were not visible, if I were not here and did not exist, then this could not have happened.

CHAPTER 8

The Service

THE THURSDAY FOLLOWING THE ACCIDENT, WE ARRIVE AT ST. CHRISTOPHER'S Episcopal Church where Elizabeth's parents are members. It is a handsome, stately structure of cream-colored brick in River Hills, a woodsy suburb north of Milwaukee. I recall our last visit five years ago for Matt and Elizabeth's wedding. On a crisp December evening, we had entered the church with joy and anticipation for the candlelight service. Now we stand in the cold, waiting for the hearse.

The funeral directors drive up and efficiently wheel out the polished walnut casket and through my mind flashes the memory of our friend Red's 1968 silver-and-black Cadillac hearse. With no children of his own, Red liked to round up a gang of neighborhood kids including Luke and Matt, who piled into the back of the vehicle to accompany him on adventures to the Frosty Tip for a treat or to the local stock car races. The kids loved these raucous outings, tumbling about in the back as Red drove them around. How different those rides from this one.

We shiver, avoid each other's eyes, and wait, unsure what else to do. A bicyclist pulls up beside the church steps. He yanks off his helmet, revealing a shaved head, slides dress pants over his black tights, then buttons himself into a white shirt. He is tall, lean, and angular. I wonder vaguely who he is. I wonder how he can bike in such frigid weather. These questions distract me until we move into the church to coalesce into a receiving line. Our line breaks apart as a tide of people surges toward us with outreached hands and hugs and tears. My face presses against men's wooly overcoats and into the crooks of perfumed necks as friends and acquaintances swaddle us in their love. Matt's college friends, teachers, childhood friends, neighbors, and grandfather's friends—they flow past us, saddened. We are surrounded by those who care about us. Crying, smiling, aching, we are awash in their love.

Some say, "I just loved Matt." Others, "I will really miss him. He was so much fun." One friend notes, "He's fishing with his grandfather now." This is comforting. Buppy had loved and nurtured Matt, taught him to fish, drive, and shoot a gun. Another friend says, "You knew his whole life," a remark which also lends comfort. No one makes the remarks I fear, such as "God needed him more than you," or "Everything happens for a reason."

Then these caring people fill the sanctuary and the overflow room with its big screen. Diffused winter light pours in from the tall, south-facing windows. The entrance music—"Ode to Joy" from Matt's favorite symphony, Beethoven's Ninth—swells forth from a small musical ensemble led by Hilary, a violinist and Matt's nursery school pal, and other young musicians she has assembled.

Fritz, Matt's cousin, reads from Ecclesiastes 3:1–8, "For everything there is a season, and a time for every matter on earth. A time to be born and a time to die . . ."

We say the Lord's Prayer and Kathy, Matt's sister-in law and a classmate since eighth grade, reads a Wordsworth poem.

My heart leaps up when I behold
A Rainbow in the sky:
So was it when my life began;
So is it now I am a man;
So be it when I shall grow old,
Or let me die!
The Child is father of the Man;
And I could wish my days to be
Bound each to each by natural piety.

I had requested to speak first so I would be finished as soon as possible with my part. While not intentional, my comments—the voice of Matt's mother—seem to set the tone for the service.

Thanks to a thoughtful middle school teacher, Matt memorized the poem you just heard. During the brief time Matt put it to memory, he was surprised to learn that I also knew it by heart. He probably thought that I was a contemporary of Wordsworth.

I am so happy that Matt learned this poem because it gave him a way to express the leaping of his heart. He was so sensitive and so appreciative of the world around him, particularly the natural world. I remember several times when we recited this together: once in a goofy way, leaping around the kitchen; another time sitting side-by-side gazing at a sunset over Green Bay; and again, indeed, watching a rainbow above a tree-rimmed lake after the rain.

"Behold" is a little used word, but I love it. It means "to feast one's eyes upon, to look one's fill." Matt did not have enough time to look his fill in this world, but the time he did have was full and rich with opportunity. He did behold much, but did not have the opportunity to grow old.

Matt was "father of the Man," in that he taught me so much, taught us so much because of the way he was able to behold the world. You each have your own memories of Matt. As his mother, I have almost thirty years full. I will cherish them and I would like to share a couple with you.

When Matt was about four our family was hiking. He was a sturdy little hiker even then. While the rest of us were looking at the trees, the ridges, and the sun, Matt, because of his close-to-the-ground viewpoint, experienced a very different hike. Because he was so close to the ground he could behold the snails. Every time he saw one, he got completely excited. He was totally delighted by them. "Here's another one!" he would shout. "There's one over here. Look at this huge, slimy one." We still have a little, framed photograph of a snail, a photo he took on that trip. The rest of us hadn't noticed the snails at all. His whole life, he helped us to behold new parts of the world.

He opened our eyes and pleased our palettes with new music and foods and philosophies, interests he closely shared with his wife, Elizabeth.

As a child, Matt plunged into things with total focus, with his full self, and he maintained this approach to life to the end. His energy, exuberance, and gusto drove his lifestyle. I remember distinctly teaching Matt to ride a bike. He would zigzag down the sidewalk, crash into a tree or fall over, and get up as fast as he could and keep on pedaling. No crying or whimpering over a scuffed knee or chin. He was intent on getting the freedom of a two-wheeled bike. I ran beside him calling out encouragement, trying to catch him when he lost his balance. That's what parents do.

I was happy and encouraging when, in more recent years, he developed a passion for biking, one the family shares. Not long ago, I began to recognize our changing roles. One moment in this transition stands out. I was fifty-four. He was nineteen. I was on a cross-country bike ride raising money for breast cancer research. Halfway through the trip in the middle of Texas, I called home to say I was giving up. Matt answered the phone and I told him I was coming home. I told him it was too hot, that the sand got in my eyes constantly because I didn't have the right glasses, and above all, I was exhausted. He said, "Mom, you aren't giving up. You have to finish. We're counting on you." How could I not keep going?

I believe God caught Matt's energetic soul last Sunday morning, the morning of the accident. I think I hear them—both Matt and God—saying to us, "Don't give up. Keep on going. I'm counting on you."

Matt himself was something to behold—from the moment of his birth. I am so grateful that I did feast my eyes upon him and his energetic life. I did not look my fill. But how can we ever do that with someone we love?

Please stand. In loving memory of Matt, please behold the people near you and give them warm hugs.

Then Kathy, Luke's wife, reads again. As stunned as the rest of our family, Kathy, nevertheless, was able to offer great support during painful days. Among our family members, I think only she possessed the strength to read the essay that Matt had written in school at the age of twelve. She reads with an unquavering voice exactly as he wrote it, omitting only the word counts he'd inserted as he worked his way to the required five hundred.

Hello. My name is Matt Manger-Lynch. I was born on September 28, 1978. My favorite animal is the penguin. I'd have one as a pet but my room would be too cold. I also like pigs and tortoises. I have a pet fish that I caught fishing Memorial Day, 1989. He eats crickets and live goldfish. He won't eat anything not alive. That is a bummer because lot's of crickets go to waste. I have a dog named Bingo. He is blind and deff, so he isn't too exciting.

When asked what would my dream house be I would probably say 30 square miles of untouched wilderness. I would not build a house or cultivate the land. I would just live off the land like an animal.

My favorite music group is Grateful Dead, even though barly anyone else my age likes them. My favorite book is Call of the Wild. My favorite movies are The Indiana Jones Trilogy.

I have traveled to Switzerland, Ecuador, the Galapagos Islands and many other places. The place I want to travel most is the USSR to see the differences and changes that are taking place.

In my free time, I play soccer very often and I like the outdoors. Soccer is my favorite sport because I feel that it is very fast moving and exciting.

My favorite class is drama because I love to act and Mrs. Sheers is very nice and funny. I also like gym class because I get to move around and not just sit at a desk.

For kindergarden I went to Milwaukee Montessori. I started school a year early because my birth date was in September and I could still be in the first grade. From there I went to New World Montessori till second grade. Then I went to Golda Meir from third grade to sixth. Now I'm here at Roosevelt and I'm loving it.

I play alto saxophone and am in the intermediat band. I played recorder for 2 years and now I have played sax for two and one half years.

Ever since I was five I was very interested in aronatics. At that age I was designing paper airplanes and from there I moved to building small roketts and launching them with esters model rocket engines. I have made a gas powered airplane on a string.   *409*

46

Every summer I go with my grandfather too Alaska. We always bring back about 70 pounds of fish each. We catch halibut (my favorite fish to eat), salmon, and lots of deep sea fish. We fly to Ketchikan and take a low flying float plane to a lodge because there are no roads.   *465*

I like to drive radio-controlled cars because I can't drive real ones. I don't have a favorite food and I will eat about anything besides liver, brussel sprouts and lima beeens. *497*

I hope I have informed you well about myself.

Elizabeth is a delicate, beautiful young woman, a psychologist and creative photographer. She stands straight and composed, rigid as a pillar. Her skin white as marble, with deep, charcoal-colored circles under her eyes, she maintains an impenetrable demeanor as she speaks with great poise of her relationship with Matt.

This I remember from her comments: "I was the rock in our marriage. I anchored the strings of Matthew, who was the kite, soaring with his great energy in so many directions. My love provided stability for him. To me he brought his free-flying self, his liveliness and drive, his humor, his passion for life, and his love."

Luke, Matt's older brother by three years and best friend since Matt's birth, stands at the steps of the altar, speaking eloquently without notes. Today he says that he cannot remember his remarks, but I do. He described Matt's zest for life, his unfettered spirit. Said Luke, "Matt took total and sheer childlike joy from very simple things in life—the taste of a burger and a beer, a favorite song played over and over, driving really fast on a country road, or calling M&M's 'Product W' and pretending it was a fancy energy food." Luke recalled that he chided Matt when he bought an expensive sports car, an Audi TT. Matt's response was, "Why should I wait until I'm fifty and I'm too old to enjoy it?"

Luke pointed out that "All of Matt's relationships were in good order, were in right alignment—with all his family and friends. Any hurts or mistakes from the past were forgiven or healed."

Lastly, "He taught us about creativity," said Luke, "about cooking and eating great food, about how to be a good friend, and how to forgive. But most of all, he taught us how to enjoy life. He was a master at it."

Bill, taking concerted effort to be strong and in control of his immense sorrow, walks slowly to the altar, shoulders slumped. His compact, wiry, athletic build—that of a triathlete in his mid-sixties—is evident even in his black suit. The lines in his high forehead are incised more deeply than a week ago. His cheekbones are sharp, dark crescents under his eyes. He has aged. His efforts to soothe and reassure the others who loved and would miss Matt are typical of his selflessness, but he is depleted.

Bill has taken seriously his role as father. As our boys matured, they came to understand him as not only a great and devoted dad, but also an admirable, principled man committed to the common good and to his community. Yet his career as a civil rights lawyer and as a volunteer for significant civic issues never took precedence over his dedication to his sons. Bill speaks and his voice is calming.

> My son Matthew did not just *touch* the lives of those gathered here, he *infused* our lives. In more ways than can be counted or articulated, he has enriched and still enriches our lives. His indomitable spirit is no longer constrained by time and space. During his life here with us he could only send one text message or e-mail at a time. He could only leave one voice mail or talk with one of us. He could only share his enthusiasm in one place at a time with only a few of us at once.

Now his spirit is freed from those limits. He can and will be with us all as our lives, as we know them, go on. Who Matt was, is part of who we are. That is a gift from Matt. That will not change. I hope that each and every one of us will take Matt along with us as we continue on life's journey.

Matt's spirit is here with us and will always be with us. He will not let us off the hook. I hope that the hearts of us all will forever be open to Matt's spirit. His spirit could not be constrained. His spirit is now free of the limits of mortal life as we know it. His boundless enthusiasm now knows no bounds.

We are all in this life together. Our lives and spirits are inextricably intertwined. We are all a part of the fabric of the lives of each of us. Matt is an uncommon thread, common to us all. Let us all rejoice.

Kathy concludes our family's part of the service by reading a poem.

> Do not weep for me, for I have lived.
> I have joined my hand with my fellows' hands,
> to leave the planet better than I found it.
> Do not weep for me, for I have loved and been loved
> by my family, by those I loved who loved me back
> for I never knew a stranger, only friends.
> Do not weep for me.
> When you reach out to touch another's heart,
> As now I touch God's face,
> I am there.
> Do not weep for me. I am not gone.
>
> -Anonymous

Scott, pastoral psychologist and retired Episcopal priest, gives encouragement, especially to the younger people in the church, by offering an explanation of death they can grasp and, possibly, even accept. He speaks about the laws of physics and the transformation of energy: that energy in one form can disappear but reappear in another form. Such is the energy of Matt, he says. It will continue to exist, but not in the way that we had known.

Then Scott, grounded guide and counselor, concludes the service: "To everything there is a season, and a time for every matter on earth. A time to be born and a time to die. Here in this last act, in sorrow, but without fear, in love and appreciation, we commit Matthew's body to its natural end."

We respond through tears: "Matthew, your life we honor, your departure we accept, and your memory we cherish."

Says Scott: "In grief at your death, but in gratitude for your life and for the privilege of sharing it with you, we commit your body to be cremated. Earth to earth, ashes to ashes, dust to dust."

We respond: "Rest now at the end of your days, your work is done. Rest in the hearts and the minds of all you love."

And Scott concludes: "Matthew, with love and respect we have been remembering your life. Your hopes and ideals we commit into our minds and wills. Your love we commit into our hearts. With these words we commit your body to its natural end."

With this blessing, we come to the end.

"It is now time for us to leave," Scott says. "May the love of friends, the radiance of memory, and the power of love fill us all with courage, strength, peace and joy; and may the grace of all that is Eternal and all that is Sacred be upon us and remain with us always. Amen."

I do not know how we can bear to follow the casket carried down the aisle by Matt's brother and friends. I feel hands reach out for us from the pews as we progress toward the light from the open church door. The weeping young men heft the box holding the body of Matthew into the hearse for the final ride.

More milling of people. More hugging, crying, and hovering around us and the photos displaying Matt at all stages of his life, each one exuding liveliness.

In the crowd I meet Nico, the cyclist I had seen arrive at the church. He quietly tells me that he had ridden that sad, freezing morning from the site of the accident in Chicago to this northern suburb of Milwaukee, a distance of about one hundred miles. Nico was the closest rider when Matt, leading the pack of cyclists, entered the intersection and was struck by the SUV. I consider asking him more questions, but conclude I am better off knowing only what I know—that Matt was doing something he loved, that he died instantly, that he did not suffer, that he could not have survived the impact.

Two years later, I was finally able to read the pages and pages of entries written about Matt on a blog site dedicated to his memory. One is Nico's: "Peace be with you, one and all. You all will be in my thoughts and in the quickness of my step as I pedal my way across this universe."

CHAPTER 9

The Chicago Ride

Two weeks after the service, on a cold Sunday in March 2008, we load our bikes on car racks to drive from Milwaukee to what is now Elizabeth's house in Chicago. Luke and Kathy have come from Wyoming and Matt's friends have come from Minneapolis and New York for this grim event. They unload their bikes into Matt's shop in the basement for some last-minute adjustments. Observing their preparations, I again change my mind and decide to ride with them. How can I miss this? Because of the cold? I have been cold since waking up this morning. I have been deadly cold for two weeks. I put on another layer—Bill's orange parka, too big—then ski gloves and a knit hat.

Like the others, I pin to my jacket the just-produced cloth patch that depicts an image of Max, the boisterous character from Maurice Sendak's *Where the Wild Things Are*, a favorite childhood book of both my sons. Under this mischievous figure who waves from his bike flows a tiny banner on which is printed: "MML 1978–2008—IN MEMORY STILL WE RIDE." The image of Max is the same one that Matt, to my dislike, had tattooed between his shoulders when he was a college freshman. Luke, in Matt's honor, followed suit after his brother's death.

The young men hoist the bikes from the basement to the alley at the side of the house. I get on my bike to follow Luke and Kathy, Bill, and sad-faced young friends. We steer out onto Chicago's icy streets bordered with hardened gray snow mounds and ride the short distance to Hamlin Park, where we wait shivering and subdued in the overcast light. Gradually, about thirty cyclists assemble, all wearing the same patch and solemn faces. Their leader, Nico, appears—hauling behind his bike a two-wheeled cart onto which is lashed a contorted, damaged bike painted stark white, tires and all.

This is not Matt's bike, which did survive the accident, but rather a ghost bike, a symbol used worldwide for the past ten years to mark places where bikers have been killed on the street. A junk bicycle painted white, the ghost bike is locked near the accident site, accompanied by a plaque bearing the date and relevant information about the rider. This honors the cyclist, serves as a grim reminder of the tragedy to passing motorists, and urges all to share the road safely with bicycles.

The Chicago police had impounded Matt's bike. Elizabeth eventually retrieved it, taking it to Yojimbo's, a small bike shop that sponsored Matt's cycling team, the Chicago Cuttin' Crew. After having it repaired, she gave the bike to a friend of Matt's. Luke did not want the bike. He had originally bought it for Matt when, like his brother and father, he became excited about biking. "This will be a great bike for you," Luke told him. It was an older, classic "Litespeed," beautiful and reasonably priced. The previous owner had upgraded everything but the titanium frame. In Matt's accident, the fork snapped in half. Two years before, Luke had suffered a serious biking accident in Jackson, Wyoming. The fork on his bike was also broken, his helmet flattened. He suffered a concussion and other injuries.

In silence we mount our bikes and in single file follow Nico and the grotesquely mangled bicycle onto North Damen Avenue. Slowly we progress through light traffic. Each pothole jars me into the reality of this scene. No cars pass, no horns honk; rather, they stop and allow passage to our sad centipede of mourners. People turn to stare at our procession. They seem to understand.

We ride several piercingly cold miles to arrive at the intersection. Keeping silence, two young men lift the crumpled bike from the cart and chain it to a rack in front of Starbucks. Luke steps forward to accept the key to the lock. They attach a white wooden sign stenciled with Matt's name and the dates of his birth and death.

Holding hands and hugging, we huddle around the bike. There is no talking, only tears. The blurred faces of family and friends and the cyclists whom I do not know surround me. I clutch to me Matt's brother and his father and hold my frozen heart.

A year after this icy ride I read an essay about Matt titled, "The Most Important Delivery I've Ever Made," written by Nico. I discovered it on the Chicago Cuttin' Crew website. It is dated March 12, 2008.

> Matt's spirit and life are certainly not embodied by just a bicycle. It was only one facet to a very layered and rich personality. This day, however, we made the most symbolic offering we could. People called people and places, and *those* people called other places and people, and everyone got together and/or contributed whatever they could to honor Matt in the best way we all knew how. Many incredible things happened that day but there was one in particular that I must share. Imagine that time you look down between your arms and look just beyond your handlebars to see . . . no one ahead of

you, nor in your peripheral. . . . The scene tricks you into believing it's just you and the bicycle while the world is off somewhere else. It's a sight we have seen and a place we have been thousands of times when each of us is out there alone on the bike. This time there was an incredible feeling I noticed as I rode and glanced down, retreating to that familiar place. I knew that even though there wasn't anyone in sight, I was not alone. This time I knew that everyone was right there with me. This time I knew Matt was right there with me.

It's a humbling experience meeting Matt's family and friends. They are incredible people who had a sense of understanding, a calm and collective wisdom. It all started with us hoping we could comfort them and in actuality, they were the strong ones comforting us.

CHAPTER 10

Shopping for Stone

IN A PALE, GRAY LAYER OF FOG, BILL AND I DRIVE WEST TO A STONE COMPANY outside the city. Bill is expressionless, hands on the wheel, jaw clenched. I concentrate on watching tears drop onto my red mittens. My heart beats fast and unevenly, and although the car is cold on this March day, I am sweating under my down coat. I have felt some urgency about this trip to order a piece of stone. My true motivation is to get my hands on anything that can alter this situation. Maybe working on the stone for Matt can wrestle back the reality I once knew.

I am numb, but thoughts of my favorite artist, Kathe Kollwitz, come to mind. Her searing images of war have stunned viewers since early in the twentieth century. When her eighteen-year-old son was killed serving as a German soldier on the Russian front in World War I, she struggled to find a way to commemorate him and the thousands of other fallen soldiers. Twenty years later, she created life-size bronze sculptures of herself and her husband—"Mourning Parents." Heads down and kneeling, these simplified, blocky figures each clutch their own bodies in grief; a gaping space looms between them. I do not want that space. I want to fill it. I want something solid there.

We park in the gray lot of a gray, stone building. Opening the glass door, we are greeted by the sound of jazz blaring a prelude to what we are about to do. Our heels click on the swirly patterned marble floor. Stone countertops, benches, walls, tables, umbrella stands, frogs, Chinese lamps, and fireplaces empty of warmth abound. There are great slabs of granite, marble, and slate—all hard, sleek, polished, and smooth. The earthy, rich colors of deep red and ochre, chocolate brown and umber, and even indigo are beribboned and flecked with contrasting pale yellow, tan, or turquoise, creating aerial-view landscapes into which I would like to disappear. Some are named for place of origin—Baltic Brown, Mesabi Black, Canadian Mist, Gold Persia, and Bordeaux. Golden Aurora and Apollo Storm simply announce their beauty. I wish we were here to choose a grand fireplace, floor tile, or a pudgy Buddha for the garden, but we have come to find the right stone for Matt.

The perky receptionist greets us from behind a stone desk, and when a salesman approaches, I unfold the piece of taped-together, brown wrapping paper on which my plan is sketched and bite the insides of my cheeks to hold my tears in check. I have worked on this design with help from Luke and Bill, and advice from my friend Susan, a stone sculptor, who suggested that our family do the carving.

We plan a stone in the form of a pup tent with one slanted side longer than the other. To prepare the drawing I rolled printer's ink with a brayer onto the soles of Matt's hiking boots, then pressed them diagonally onto the paper, transferring the pattern of the tread of his boots. Two of the footprints will be fully on the face of the stone; only the heel of the third will be visible in the upper corner. The stone company will engrave his footprints on the front face of the stone—Matt striding onto, then off of—the face of the earth. On the short ends of the stone, beneath engravings of large-mouth bass will be the dates of his life: 1978–2008. On the vertical front edge, inspired by his essay, Matt's words: "Here is my dream home." On the slanted back face of the stone we will carve flowing lines resembling moving currents of water into which our tears and rain will flow.

The knowledgeable salesman, stone-faced himself, studies the drawing, not indicating that our design differs from others he encounters in the course of a day. I am grateful for his businesslike, taciturn manner. He says little, making only terse comments and asking just a few questions, such as, "Is it twenty-eight inches along this side?" I remember him saying, "Yes, limestone will be the easiest to carve." Quickly, we choose a beautiful piece, fine-textured and ivory white. We leave in dull silence.

CHAPTER 11

Carving Stone

IN LATE MARCH 2008, SUSAN CALLS TO SAY THE STONE COMPANY DELIVERED the stone to her studio and that it awaits us. She has prepared a place for us to work in the studio, a chubby brown barn once a chicken coop. It is a peaceful site for our sad task.

On the east side of Susan's barn, patches of dry, golden grass emerge from snowdrifts in random patterns. Cardinals and woodpeckers flit around birdhouses and feeders rising above the dried stems and stalks of last summer's garden. Behind the barn stretches a snowy wetland etched with winter's stark trees.

I recall a party Susan hosted many years ago. It now seems a dream. She invited friends to go skating on a Sunday afternoon after a heavy winter rain followed by a sudden freeze had transformed the wetland into a glistening ice rink. A breeze had drifted the light snow close to the tree trunks, leaving the ice between clean and smooth. Matt and Luke—at the time little boys dressed in bulky snow pants, heavy jackets, hats, and mittens—took to the ice like two unleashed puppies, speeding and sashaying about, teetering on the slick surface, then gliding along, disappearing behind trees, then emerging. Bill and I followed them—meeting then parting, whirling about, falling, skidding—as we cut across the shimmering reflections of trees and skimmed along on this endless rink. Today, the wetland is only a bleak background for the little barn. So much has changed.

Under the barn's eaves and above its entrance, a pair of white, weathered antlers reaches out to those stooping to enter. To the right, under a pine tree towering protectively over the barn, a rusty metal lawn chair seems to be waiting for Matt to supervise our project. Were he here he might simply say, "Hi, folks. What's up?" and delight in surprising us. He'd be wearing his gray wool jacket, his arms folded across his chest, legs extended straight out, ankles crossed, slouching comfortably. His knit hat pulled to his eyebrows would just reveal his dark eyes, full of fun. But, he is not here.

Some days after Susan's call, in the chilling, dismal part of Wisconsin's winter, our small group—Bill and I; Elizabeth, her sister, brother, and parents, Bob and Jane; and Matt's friend David—squeeze into the tiny studio to observe Susan's quick demonstration on the basics of carving. Our faces are yellow-gray and somber in the morning light filtering through the dusty windows. Fine, white marble dust has sifted onto all of the room's surfaces—the brown plastic radio, wooden shelves, and brick floor—and settled indelibly into its walls during the twenty years Susan has worked here. Sculptures still partly contained by solid blocks of stone are stacked in the corners, and marble chunks not yet touched by the artist stand here and there. Curling out from the wall are yellowed newspaper articles, reviews, photos, and posters of Carrara, Italy, where Susan studied and buys her marble. A gnarled section of an oak tree leans scepter-like in one corner; collections of weathered bones and bits of nature clutter the shelves.

We gather around Susan and the stone. Fine, white powder lies in a silky layer on Susan's skin, haloes her hair, and bleaches her blue jacket.

This woman of great heart is a skilled and accomplished sculptor. Decades of carving stone have developed her muscular arms and hands. She explains how to use the hammers, points, and chisels with simple instructions. "Hold the steel point in one hand and tap it with the hammer. Do this over and over as you point in the direction you want the cuts to go." She deftly demonstrates on a separate piece of stone, her movements full of power and grace. She hands the tools to Elizabeth, who tentatively taps then drops her hands heavily to her sides. It is a task too sad. We each, in turn, heft the tools and attempt to follow the lines I have drawn in black crayon on the white surface.

When the others leave, I stay to do a mother's work. Near the peak of the stone, I position the point and tap its end with the hammer, but not even a tiny impression results. Although the stone is softer than marble and supposedly easier to carve, when I whack it with the point there is no give. The "soft" limestone is impenetrable and unyielding, formed from shells and fossils laid down over millions of years at the bottom of the inland sea that covered the Midwest. Under enormous pressure and movement of the earth, it gradually hardened. I am aware of my own hardening, also caused by the shifts and changes in my part of the earth.

With a gulp of air, I take up the point and the hammer and begin again. I finally succeed in cutting several dents that begin the bands of rivulets I hope to create. Eventually I am able to tap down the flowing stream of lines, hatching out tiny chunks. I am seeking a rhythm, trying to sense what the tools and the stone are telling me. I am also chipping away at my grief. My tears slide down the shallow grooves. Perhaps they can soften the angular edges of my crude carving.

I had planned to work all day, but after several hours my shoulders, elbows, and hands are throbbing. Even with the space heaters glowing, the studio is cold, so I work in hat, jacket, and gloves. Protective glasses pinch my temples and the facemask is smothering and uncomfortable. This challenge is greater than I had imagined, but my action is movement toward honoring my son and healing myself.

In the following weeks, I work on the stone whenever I can dredge up the courage to emerge from my cave of sorrow and undertake this heartbreaking effort. Some days, brave and caring friends lend a hand. With their help, the meandering lines deepen and lengthen, working their way down the slanted face of the limestone.

Carving is harsh and jarring. But the next phase, the sanding and polishing, is mesmerizing, soothing. I smooth down the grainy roughness, layer by thin layer, as I slide the sandpaper back and forth, back and forth. In the rhythmic daze of sanding, I am tempted to persist until I reduce the entire stone to dust. In time to my polishing, I sing old Bob Dylan songs that Matt used to laugh at, but liked. The steady friction refines the ripples and slightly softens my pain.

I do not want to stop; the momentum is tranquilizing, therapeutic. I imagine, unrealistically, that if I can maintain this rhythm indefinitely the inevitable conclusion—moving the stone to its resting place—will not happen, and we will not have to again acknowledge Matt's death.

My fingertips are nearly sanded away and raw when I become aware that the satiny, flowing water approximates what I had imagined. I step back for a critical look. The carved side of the stone looks slightly primitive and more rugged than I had expected, the curves more angular than flowing. Rough-cut marks remain in certain deeply etched sections. Overall, this seems appropriate and fitting for Matt.

I lean forward and touch my cheek to the cold, furrowed, and still-powdery surface. I run my hands along the water-like ridges following the lines we have created. Leaning against the stone, I reach my hands around to the front and slide my fingers over Matt's boot prints. Flattening my hands against the sides, I touch the impressions of the bass. Reluctantly releasing my hold on the stone, I straighten and stand. "Matt will like this," I say aloud.

CHAPTER 12

Ghost Bike

WHILE WE WERE CARVING THE STONE, IN CHICAGO ELIZABETH HAD A different concern. On May 22, 2008, she was dismayed to see a photograph of the ghost bike on the front page of the Metro section of the *Chicago Tribune*. Taken at the intersection of the accident, it showed the white, crumpled bike still chained in front of Starbucks. The sign bearing Matt's name and the date of his death was starkly visible. The article, "Ethereal Reminder of the Road's Dangers," was subtitled "Across city, ghostly white bikes stand as memorials to cyclists who have been killed in car accidents."

I am grateful to Elizabeth and admire her courage. While we lamented this published reminder of Matt's death, she decided to remove the sign. The reminder of his death had been public for sufficient time. Four months later, just days before Matt's birthday, Elizabeth would send out an e-mail explaining that decision.

Subject: I have removed Matt's nameplate

I have made a decision to remove Matthew's nameplate from the ghost bike. It is very important to me that Matt's spirit be untethered from the notion of violence that is associated with that spot. I believe that removing his name will accomplish this. His spirit needs to roam and rest in peace; to be allowed to fully connect with all the freedom, beauty, and fun that exist in the universe. I understand that the ghost bike serves a purpose for the community and I am not asking for the bike to be taken down. Just his name, his calling card. Thank you for respecting this decision during this painful and challenging time in my life.

CHAPTER 13

A Visit to Chicago

"Look for a beat-up, dark blue Honda," Matt's friend Stephanie had said in her e-mail invitation to visit the Chicago where her life and Matt's had intersected. I spot her as I emerge from Union Station into the breezy June air. I have not seen her since the funeral, four months ago. She leans over to open the passenger door, and I am struck once again by her brown-black eyes, shining and soft, so big and compelling that it takes a while to notice anything else about her. Today, they fill with tears as she smiles and welcomes me. She has a plan, thoughtfully considered, to give me a view of part of Matt's recent life.

The back seat cradles a jumble of platters, pans, candles, random flowers, potholders, and containers of various shapes, colors, and sizes, her gear for Mandoline, the catering company that she and Matt had shared. Everything rattles and clunks as we head to the Outer Drive, the expressway that follows the shoreline of Lake Michigan. We stop briefly for Stephanie to point out the bike path where Matt had ridden most mornings—about forty miles daily. "Why couldn't he have kept riding here?" she asks in a soft

69

voice. I look at the path, the happy, intent bikers spinning along it, the lake sparkling behind them.

In Chicago, Matt first worked at the restaurant Trio, then Ambria, where he was *chef de poissonier.* When Ambria closed, he worked with Stephanie at Mandoline, began teaching himself the art of charcuterie, and contemplated his next career move.

Stephanie and Matt had met in college, through a girlfriend of Stephanie's who was dating both him and another boy named Matt. To distinguish between the two, the girls called our Matt "curly-haired Matt." A year ahead of him at Macalester College, Stephanie had also worked for Hadj at the Barbary Fig. When she left for La Grenouille in New York, Matt attended her going-away party. "Hadj prepared lamb's brains and balls, which we ate outside after work one summer night while listening to Stevie Wonder," she recalled. Later, when her internship at La Grenouille ended, she contacted Matt to fill her spot. It was a significant training ground for both.

Mandoline's main client was a monthly eating club affiliated with the University of Chicago that met in a rented space at the Hyde Park Union Church and drew between twenty-five and forty-five diners. Stephanie said Mandoline had "something of a cult following in the neighborhood." Today she describes a dinner she and Matt had prepared featuring a whole pig, serving different parts of the animal for each course, one of which included headcheese. Another memorable meal, *salmon en croute,* a whole salmon Matt wrapped in brioche dough, she recalls as "visually spectacular and delicious."

After Matt died, there was an interlude during which meetings were suspended while Stephanie recovered, regrouped, and hired a couple of helpers. When the meetings resumed, club members held a meal in honor of Matt at which Stephanie served preserved lemons he had made.

The day I visit, Stephanie is preparing food for a wedding Mandoline is catering. "I thought it would be nice for both of us to spend some time cooking together," explains Stephanie. "Matt would have helped a lot with this wedding so it is nice that you can help instead. I also find it helpful to keep one's hands busy—especially busy with food or something else nurturing—during times of grief. This is why I am glad you could come work with me."

I stand in the "cooking room" (a gas stove surrounded tightly on three sides by stainless steel walls) of the little kitchen that Stephanie and Matt had rented in what was once a corner carryout joint in the modest Bridgeview neighborhood southwest of Chicago. With a crepe pan in each hand, I follow Stephanie's directions. My sweat and tears drip and flow, but I soon sense that the rhythm of pouring the batter, watching for the right moment, flipping, and then removing the crepes from the pans is completely engaging and soothing. Pour, watch, wait, flip, wait, remove—over and over. "That'll do it," Stephanie says when the stacks on the Formica counter behind me tower three hundred crepes high. The next day she will fill them with goat cheese, chicken in a creamy, herb-tomato sauce, and spinach. I imagine how Matt would have peered over my shoulder to make a witty comment or give me subtle and humorous words of advice; he might have been proud of his mom, who had never before made crepes.

At noon we go to Gio's, a neighborhood Italian deli where Stephanie and Matt sometimes ate. There, we watch craggy-faced, Italian-speaking men sit beneath a layer of cigarette smoke at tables covered in red-and-white-checked cloths sipping espresso. As we spoon rich *pasta e fagiole* soup from wide, white bowls, I scan the shelves stacked with Italian specialty items, an array of pastas, instant coffee, and toilet paper. I can see why Matt liked this cozy place.

Stephanie tells me about sitting, after work, in the wine cellar Matt had built in the basement of his and Elizabeth's house. Luke called this Matt's "man cave." Here the usually spontaneous Matt became completely organized and meticulous. He had educated himself on subjects ranging from biodynamic grape cultivation to obscure French vintners. He neatly labeled each bottle, which he had carefully purchased from random lots. Surrounded by the beginning of a collection, he and Stephanie relaxed and reviewed their catering events, drank red wine, and savored bits of the smoky meat and sausage he had cured.

I travel home on the train, devouring Mandoline's rich, molten chocolate cake, soothed by it, and nourished by Stephanie's loving efforts to cheer me.

CHAPTER 14

Upper Peninsula Gathering

ON A HOT THURSDAY IN JULY SIX MONTHS AFTER MATT'S DEATH, BILL AND I charge into the Dollar Store in the town of L'Anse in Upper Michigan. The northern of two land masses that constitute the state of Michigan, the Upper Peninsula is wooded, wildly beautiful, lined with pristine rivers, sparsely populated, and undeveloped. In this remote, untamed landscape, Matt sought refuge from the scramble of the city.

After a long drive, we are feeling out of sorts, edgy, and exhausted. The smells of cheap fabric, plastic, and caramel corn permeating the store are nauseating. Fluorescent lights are blinking and a scratchy loudspeaker repeatedly announces the specials of the afternoon. We are searching for markers for the obscure twists and turns on the road that friends and family will follow to our cabin on Saturday.

Bill heads down one aisle and I, another. We meet in the toy department and decide on brightly colored, plastic pinwheels on sticks. We buy twelve and chuck them into our car, already full of coolers, beer, bulging grocery sacks, duffel bags, and Matt's stone, which occupies a third of the space. Its sacred presence in the midst of picnic paraphernalia is a haunting reminder of the reason for our trip.

A short distance up the highway, a few miles south of the Lake Superior shore, we turn onto a road that passes a small cemetery I once found charming. The pavement turns to dirt and the forest closes around us. The potholes in the road are full from the previous night's rain. As we bump and careen through them, sprays of mud pelt the car. Hacked tree stumps and enormous boulders, heaved up from the earth when the road was cut, hold the deep and craggy forest in place. In contrast, graceful ferns arch around rocks and trees, softening the intersection between nature and man's intrusion upon it.

Our drive ends south of Lake Superior at the edge of a small lake, a secluded body of water circled by trees. The cabin is still there, standing stalwartly, waiting. I see Matt, or wish I did, alone with his fishing rod at the end of the rickety dock, also waiting.

I cannot spend time thinking about him now because we have to prepare for the weekend. I put him out of mind for the time being. A beautiful gray canoe, treasured by Matt, fills the floor space of the cabin's main room. Bill and I carry it outside and down to the dock. While Bill directs his attention to the generator and hooks up the gas, I sweep away cobwebs, and slide open windows to air out the dust and smell of mildew. I unload groceries and other gear.

Near the side door is a bucket half-filled with water, our "UP mousetrap." A small wooden plank angles from the floor to the bucket's edge. Written on the plank in Matt's slanted handwriting is a note of feigned encouragement to the doomed pests: "Stairway to heaven. Leap. Go for it." Above the water's surface, a beer can hangs horizontally from a wire stretching across the top of the bucket. Peanut butter spread on the can entices hungry mice to make the leap from the top of the plank. When their tiny feet land on the can they begin a deadly spin and eventually plummet into the bucket.

Before the sun sets, Bill and I walk the familiar, overgrown path that circles the lake, crossing the arched wooden bridge over the outflow creek that meanders away into a swamp directly across the lake from the cabin. Then we plod up a hill. At its crest is a level clearing in the trees, a fire ring at its center and a stack of firewood at its edge. We are silent, remembering Matt's love for this spot, how he camped here with his friends and brother. I imagine them laughing and drinking, the firelight touching their young faces, and later, lying in sleeping bags as the fire's red embers fade into darkness, stars overhead.

On one side of the clearing is a small glade, the perfect spot for the stone. Here, small birch trees will shelter it, and tall white pines will stand sentinel above it. Over the years, it will grow gray and green with lichen and moss, and will take on a smudgy patina as it merges into this wild environment. In fall, the bright leaves of maple and birch will color the clearing's floor. Chipmunks and squirrels will scurry nearby, perhaps jumping to the peak of the stone for a better view of their terrain. White tail deer, moose, bear, wolves, raccoons, and fox will pass by with nary a glance. The winter snow, well over two hundred inches a year in this northern climate, will bury it. Hawks, osprey, woodpeckers, eagles, and chickadees will fly over it.

Bill and I stand at this high point looking out over the early evening lake, certain that this is the place to nestle the memory of Matt.

CHAPTER 15

Placing the Stone

THE GATHERING ACTUALLY BEGINS FRIDAY WHEN LUKE FLIES IN FROM Wyoming. Kathy will come the following day. Matt's childhood friend David arrives on the overnight bus from Milwaukee to Houghton, Michigan, where we meet him. He regales us with stories of his journey through the night, including an arrest on the bus, and descriptions of the characters he encountered. He comes for support, to support us, and to remember Matt.

There is work to do. Knee-high grass and wildflowers nearly hide the path around the lake. Luke wields the "brush hog" in a dual ritual of "clearing away" and "clearing the way." He says he feels good spending these hours moving the brush cutter rhythmically back and forth in a meditative state, watching for rocks as he absorbs the vibrations of the engine.

In the afternoon, Luke, Bill, and David prepare a place for the stone. They level the ground, dig several inches down into the earth, then fill the depression with buckets of sand. They tamp it down and shovel in gravel to create a firm base. When they finish, I overhear the manly discussion on strategies for moving the two hundred-pound stone to the four-wheeler and then to the campsite. Should they drive up the shorter, steeper route or take the longer way around the lake affording a more gradual ascent? Eventually they make a ramp with weathered planks, slide the stone out of the car, and ease it onto the back of the chubby, four-wheeled vehicle. Luke drives off slowly while Dave and Bill walk alongside, bracing the stone. The engine fades as they slowly circle the lake. I am not yet ready to see the stone replace Matt in this, his favorite spot.

On Saturday morning, the eagle nesting near the lake swings over-head, signaling the start of a day of sadness and recognition. I do ordinary preparations as though for any summer picnic, tasks that occupy and distract me. I root around in the musty cupboards and pull out the motley collection of kitchen equipment. I make salads, butter buns, and set out plastic bowls, platters, paper plates, and napkins. These mundane actions, ritualistic and reassuring, are a soothing prelude to the afternoon event. I dump bags of ice into coolers filled with beer—unusual pale ales, stout, and others Matt favored. I gather field daisies, still dewy, and arrange them in big pickle jars filled with lake water. As the sun rises up over the trees, Bill and I carry the flowers to the site and arrange them around the stone. Where the path opens out to the campsite we bend small saplings, twine them together, and twist in bunches of daisies and ferns. When we release the saplings they spring upward to form a flowery archway, a graceful entrance to this sacred space.

As the day reaches perfection with gentle breezes and clear skies, others arrive: Matt's favorite Uncle Bob and Aunt Betsy; Fritz and Dylan, his cousins from California; Elizabeth and her parents, Dr. Bob and Jane; his best friend Nick and childhood friend Micah, both from Minneapolis; Mike, Irene, and other friends who have driven long distances. They have known Matt as a child and as an adult. It begins.

I go first to the site, lugging a huge brass-centered Chinese *chao* gong Matt gave me. The gong pings and whispers as twigs and ferns along the path gently brush against it. Touching a gong brings fortune and strength, say the Chinese. I need such strength now.

I lean the gong against a white pine, then stand in this quiet place, waiting. Shortly, I hear the little motorboat coming across the lake and the sound of the cousins' voices talking above its drone. To my left, the solemn procession of friends and family quietly emerges from the woods and crosses the wooden bridge. Some bear flowers from their gardens, and sunflowers—which Matt loved. I lose sight of them as they follow the path through the trees and up the hill. They reappear at the crest, stooping slightly to pass under the delicate arbor and lay down their floral offerings in front of the stone.

In silence, we form a semicircle. In a hesitant voice, Bill welcomes everyone and invites them to speak. But what can we say? The funeral service has already happened. This is not a burial. We hoped it would be a day of recognition, of healing and honoring, a day of remembering and putting to rest.

Matt's father-in-law, whom we affectionately call "Dr. Bob," is a caring, kindly fellow who loved Matt and shared his passion for great food and cooking. He begins to speak, but his tears interfere. Luke reads, but I am unable to comprehend. I read a Pueblo blessing I found during months of frenzied reading trying to understand the death of our young son, but I can't seem to hear my own voice.

Pueblo Blessing
Hold on to what is good
Even if it is a handful of earth
Hold on to what you believe
Even if it is a tree that stands by itself
Hold on to what you must do

Even if it is a long way from here
Hold on to life
Even if it is easier to let go
Hold on to my hand
Even if I have gone away from you

Others speak, although I can't absorb what they are saying. I am teary, out of focus in this place of great beauty and great sorrow. Standing at the edge of the bluff, Nick, Matt's good friend from college days, then suspends the gong by its cord. I only glimpse his red face and tears as I begin to swing the beater. The white cotton tip strikes the brass center. I sound the gong for each year of Matt's life. Each strike elicits a deep, sonorous burst, creating a wave-like succession of tones from deep to shrill. The rainbow of sounds echoes from the hill, resonates out across the lake, out to the universe, it seems. I swing and count, my ears booming with the reverberations— twenty-five, twenty-six, twenty-seven, twenty-eight.

"Look," someone says. I look up just before the last stroke. On the opposite shore two deer, startled by the din, have burst from the woods. They skitter and dance in place, bound and splash through shallow water along the shore. Then, with light-footed grace, they leap into the shelter of the woods.

I strike twenty-nine. We watch and listen in awe and sorrow as the gong's vibrations again echo across the water. Several minutes pass. Quiet returns and settles over us.

Ducking under the arbor, we wend our way down the path, maiden-hair ferns brushing legs and fingertips. At the base of the hill, we cluster at the lake's edge where wispy grasses touched by a quiet breeze slice arcs in the water. Luke holds the sturdy paper packet of Matt's ashes. Designed to biodegrade, this six-by-six-by-two-inch package is tastefully constructed of handmade paper, embedded with bits of pastel-colored leaves and flowers, and tied with an ivory, paper ribbon. We selected it from a catalogue of variously shaped containers for human ash. This one, marketed to the sensibilities of environmentally concerned grievers, seemed a better choice than those in the form of Grecian urns, dogs, or bowling balls. We had no interest in keeping Matt's remains on our mantel.

Luke crouches on the wet pebbles to give the packet a gentle nudge, releasing the precious vessel to float away from shore, away from us. I hold my breath as the breeze snags it, whisks it lightly across the surface, and releases it to execute a graceful descent into the tannin-tinged water. I imagine it beneath the surface, swaying and spiraling through the copper-gold water, ushered by wands of sunlight. The light ribbon binding the packet unfurls in slow motion, freeing the ashes and small remnants of bone—femur, clavicle, and ear bone—to swirl and drift, suspended in a delicate descending cloud of gray before sinking to land on rocks and muddy lake bottom. Curious bass appear to inspect, and then welcome, the arrival of a friend.

CHAPTER 16

The Picnic

SILENCE HOLDS ON THE TREK BACK TO THE CABIN WHERE THE YOUNG MEN immediately open the beer that Micah, lifetime friend from our neighborhood, and Nick, college buddy, have brought from the Surly Brewery in Minneapolis. The offerings include Matt's favorites—labeled Furious, Bender, and Cynic. There is much attention to food, as Matt would have had it. Nick circles around the small kitchen carefully preparing aromatic sauerkraut the way Matt had taught him, simmering it with bacon and beer until all moisture evaporates, then adding a handful of caraway seed.

Nick and Micah had driven miles out of their way to the tiny town of Fifield, Wisconsin, to purchase bratwurst from a family grocery that was a favorite of Matt's. He had loved buying directly from the sausage-making owner, had taken great delight in discussing the process with him, and had a particular passion for eating the varieties of bratwurst—cranberry, potato, sauerkraut, and bacon—made there. Clearly, despite his Cordon Bleu culinary education and his experiences cooking and eating in great restaurants, Matt was not a food snob. He had an exuberant and infectious enthusiasm for good food of any kind, from fried cheese curds to truffles.

While coals glow in the grills and brats begin to hiss and spatter, there is drinking and merriment, not false, but clearly brought about with concerted and valiant effort. We strive to create a time that Matt would have enjoyed, but we cannot make up for his absence. He was usually the spark igniting any event.

Elizabeth and Luke, widow and grieving brother, row the little fishing boat out into the lake. Again, the breeze cooperates; this time it hoists Matt's big parafoil kite aloft as Elizabeth and Luke grip the handles attached to the kite's lines.

The wind lifts the kite. It swoops gracefully upward, rising above the boat, each of its separate cells of lightweight, rip-stop fabric swelling, each blazing its own color—red, orange, yellow, blue, green, violet. We cheer from the deck as the rainbow-colored, U-shaped kite arcs, dips, and soars. My heart leaps up.

Matt had been an ardent fisherman, catching fish carefully and gently releasing hundreds in this lake. So the younger men and Kathy, an expert fisherwoman, have a hand at fishing from the boat and dock before the sun sets. Matt had intended to teach his friend Nick to fish. Nick is an urbane, handsome young man who works for the Bank of Canada. Matt was an outdoorsman. Yet their energy levels were equally intense, as were their interests in food, cooking, wine, and football. They also shared a similar sense of humor. Today, Nick is dressed neatly for outdoor activities. Luke had told him to bring a tent and to everyone's delight he brought his five-year-old son's pink-and-yellow Dora the Explorer tent. He shares in the laughter over this.

In Matt's place, Luke becomes Nick's guide. They climb into the little boat and Luke rows across the smooth, darkening lake to a spot near the middle where he knows they will get at least some bites. He expertly casts his spin rod. "Like this, Nick," he coaches. Nick does a good imitation of Luke's cast and immediately has a bite. He is ecstatic, shouting so that everyone onshore can hear. "I caught one! I caught one!" In a few minutes, he hollers again. "I caught two! I caught two!" Nick continues to blare out his count until he catches seven large- and smallmouth bass. Maybe Matt was helping his friend experience one of his own favorite pastimes.

The smoky beckoning of cooked bratwurst draws everyone to fill their plates, and as we eat, the sun disappears behind the campsite across the lake, now the home of Matt's stone.

Then come the stories. And this evening, like many others in the past, Matt entertains us, although he is present only in our hearts and in spirit. "On a fishing trip in Canada," begins Matt's Uncle Bob, my brother, struggling for composure.

> Matt was about eleven at the time. One afternoon after a full day of fishing, I headed over to the bar for a beer. As I walked in, there was Matt, perched on a bar stool between two seasoned fishermen, listening to them complain about their bad luck that day.
> One of the guys turned to Matt and said, "How about you, kid? How'd your day go? Catch anything?" Matt didn't pause. "I got one every cast," he lied, a big grin on his face.

The story became a family legend. In fact, we used Matt's quote on the back of the program for his service along with a photo of him as a young man holding up a bass and smiling broadly.

Bob begins another story. By the end, he is laughing through his tears.

> When Matt was fourteen I took him on a guided turkey hunt on the Rosebud Sioux Reservation near Wounded Knee, South Dakota. I couldn't believe it:

Matt shot the two turkeys his permit allowed on the first morning! To get a new permit, we tracked down the chief, finding him at a local gas station. Matt then went out and shot two more turkeys, the last one on the morning of his flight home. We went into the tiny Rapid City airport with Matt gripping his most recent victim—a twenty-pound bird—by the neck. (This was before the days of heightened airport security.) A group of hunters waiting for flights stared in awe. None of them had bagged a turkey. Matt wasn't a kid to brag, but when these guys in camouflage asked about his hunt, he answered: "This is the fourth one I got." Their eyes bugged out and their jaws dropped. Our guide seized the moment and passed out a handful of his business cards.

Bob took one of my favorite photos of Matt on that trip. His beaming face emerges from his camouflage getup and the brush surrounding him. He hoists a big dark turkey; more lie beside him. This was a moment of sheer, male adolescent joy. Bob has since returned to hunt with the same guide, who boasts that Matt still holds the record for the most turkeys shot on a weekend hunt.

Eating, drinking, crying, laughing, we remember Matt. And I remember a prayer from Matt's service.

> In the rising of the sun and in its going down,
>   we will remember Matt.
> Spirit of Love, hear our prayer.
> When we notice things he liked,
>   we will remember Matt.
> Spirit of Love, hear our prayer.
> When we see in others glimpses of his ways,
>   we will remember Matt.
> Spirit of Love, hear our prayer.

When we see in ourselves things
  that he would value,
  we will remember Matt.
Spirit of Love, hear our prayer.
So long as we live, Matt will live in us,
  as we remember him.
Spirit of Love, hear our prayer.
In the midst of our grief,
  we seek the comfort of one another's love.
Spirit of Love, hear our prayer.
May we find comfort and richness
  in our memories of Matt.
Spirit of Love, hear our prayer.
Thank you, Matt, for the good times.
Thank you for your love and your laughter.
Most of all, thank you for being you.
You leave this world a better place
  than you found it.
Spirit of Love, hear our prayer.

Later that night, the younger members of the group sit at the campsite beside a campfire and Matt's stone. Eventually, it's only the men who remain: Luke, David, and Nick, drinking and telling stories. Matt is with them. Later, Luke described that night.

> The fire pit there was small and so we put lots of little pine sticks on it. There's something instinctually relaxing for men to sit and drink around a fire in the woods at night that can't be described. I'm sure it's got something to do with cavemen. It's just the easiest thing to be around good friends, when you can say absolutely whatever, and you know it doesn't matter.
> The fire bounced light off the trees and the frogs chirped below, and it just seemed like Matt should

have shown up at anytime. If he had, he would have had some wild enthusiasm. Some idea of something he wanted to do—something we could talk about and plan. Something he hadn't done before. He always had some spark, especially there in the woods—that certain way of making an ordinary sandwich exciting, or the way a road trip turned into an adventure. How empty it felt to have him gone.

I told those guys about the last time I had been there with Matt. It was late September. It was rainy, cold, and windy the whole time. At first, we had some chores to do to fill the time—we got the new stove, puttered around with the chainsaw. But the weather was driving us nuts. We needed to do something fun, exciting. On the last day the wind was howling out of the west. Matt and I suited up in heavy rubber raincoats and rubber boots and rowed out on the lake in the whitecaps to go fishing. We had learned that the fish were deeper than normal and we anchored off the rocky point on the north side of the lake. One of us had to row to keep the boat in place while the other cast. We laughed and laughed. Drank coffee, and cast and cast. Amazingly, we caught some nice smallmouth. We knew that neither of us would have had any luck convincing any of our friends to go fishing that day, even for a minute. But neither of us really had talked the other into it. We just knew it was the right thing to do that day—to go out and see how it went.

As we talked about Matt, I stared at the light flickering off the stone monument, thinking how solid and permanent it was. How with a shovel, some scoops of sand and gravel, and a little sweat we had made it so the stone would sit there basically forever. It would survive a forest fire, a tornado, a thousand winters. Unlike a human life. How fragile we all are. Matt was proof of that.

The mood around the fire—I don't know how to describe it—soulful, perhaps. Wistful. We all tried really hard to have fun, to laugh. We knew Matt would want that for us. So I guess I'd say we were trying. And partially succeeding. That special place was filled with love and positive energy. And, maybe that night was one of those rare instances from those days that reminded me that life goes on.

CHAPTER 17

A Second Visit to Chicago

I RETURN TO CHICAGO IN DECEMBER 2008. IT'S BEEN ABOUT SIX MONTHS since my visit there with Stephanie and nearly a year since the accident. This time I am traveling with Alison, a young family friend. We rush to catch the 8:00 a.m. train from Milwaukee to Chicago. The temperature is nineteen degrees below zero. Layers of gray mist rise from steely Lake Michigan as we head to the train station. While I park, Alison runs to get tickets and we meet in the straggly line of passengers moving toward the track. Once in our seats we chat and drink coffee, but do not mention Matt.

Elizabeth meets us at Union Station, smiling and happy. She is radiantly beautiful. I have always understood why Matt fell in love with her. Her smile, composure, creativity, and intelligence are only part of it. She is also artistically talented, sensitive, grounded, and determined. She waves hello and we jump into her car, headed for a day of shopping. Our first stop is the paper store to buy a journal for a memorial shelter that we plan to build along the North Country National Scenic Trail in Michigan's Upper Peninsula in honor of Matt. I look over the journals while Elizabeth and Alison admire cards, papers, and doodads, giggling like carefree girls. Most of the journals are too frivolous or flowery or have "Guests" or "Wedding Day" embossed on their covers, not appropriate for the wilderness. I find a brown leather-covered book, sturdy and rugged, like Matt. It will hold up under the hands of tired hikers stopping for the night. Alison and Elizabeth find just the right pens for writing in the journal.

We spend the morning in a number of stores that Elizabeth knows of. At one, they help me pick out a big, warm coat, then finger and sift through the endless racks of clothing. Each has her preferences: Elizabeth has a keen fashion eye and can zoom in on great, stylish garments. Anything would look good on her. Alison is attracted to the quirky and whimsical. We try on goofy hats in Bloomingdale's. I am drawn to a pink suede, tie-dyed number that changes me into an elf for only $700. "Who wears these?" I ask, holding up a pair of six-inch-high stiletto heels that I consider instruments of torture. "I do," they both say, laughing. I am fortunate to share the day with these young, blooming women who seem unaware of the men passing by who turn their heads to take a second or third look. I am the *dueña*—the elder, the guardian—who accompanies and protects these beauties from harm. This, despite the fact that they may think they watch over me.

These moments are carefree, happy except for a gripping pang of sadness now and then. It lurks between moments of pleasure. I am glad Elizabeth and Alison can hold tight to their sorrow and still enjoy the world. For them, spending this day together is nothing special, but for me it is a time when I touch Matt.

Elizabeth takes us to see her new apartment. It is compact, cozy, and white with sunshine streaming in from skylights. It is comfortable—for two. She lives with her partner, Nathan, a chef who was a friend of Matt. She leads us upstairs and down, directing our attention to this or that. As I pass a small bookcase, I spot the thick, leather-bound copy of *Larousse*

Gastronomique, the classic French guide to cooking everything, which I bought for Matt at a secondhand store. I gave it to him at the start of his cooking days, and remember his surprise and smile when I handed it to him. I am glad that Elizabeth has kept it.

Later, on the train ride home, Alison tells me that she also saw a cookbook she had given to Matt. Resting my forehead against the cool glass window and watching the frigid landscape, I think that this is as it should be. Elizabeth is young. She needs to fold away her loss, live in the present, and create a new life for herself without Matt.

CHAPTER 18

First Anniversary

THE HAPPY DAY OF MATT'S BIRTH IS WHAT I WANT TO REMEMBER, BUT ON February 24, 2009, I begin to sink. This e-mail from his lifelong childhood friend arrives, indicating we were of like minds.

> Hi guys,
>
> I know that all of our hearts are heavy today, as it has been one year since Matt left us. It has been a difficult and agonizingly long year. I think that Matt's birthday is a better anniversary—the date I prefer to observe. However, I know that we are all painfully aware of the significance of 2/24. I just wanted to reach out and let you all know that you are all in my thoughts today. I wish you strength and happiness in the days to come.
>
> With love,
> David

On this somber anniversary, our family (minus one) needs to be together. Luke organizes a trip to commemorate the date. He was inspired by an adventure of Matt's eleven years earlier. Facing self-doubt and troubled times during his sophomore year of college, Matt had taken a semester off. He came home, worked at a bagel joint, and tried to reorient himself. He decided a physical challenge might help him and made an Outward Bound trip his goal, saving money to help with the cost. Cross-country skiing and dogsledding in the Boundary Waters of northern Minnesota in January might sound like torture to some, but were attractive to Matt. His letters, in his slanted, bold handwriting, reveal that he rediscovered his exuberance and zest for life on this trip. In a letter dated January 16, 1998, he not only described its challenges, but also included little drawings of dogs and an intricate rendering of a sled he had just lashed together.

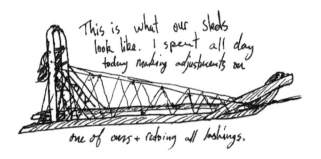

This is what our sleds look like. I spent all day today making adjustments on one of ours + redoing all lashings.

The days are pretty fun, cross-country skiing, pulling small sleds full of gear, called pulks. Most of the time is spent on rivers or lakes, some portages. Today we learned how to hook up dogs and go sledding with them. That's pretty fun, the dogs are pretty rambunctious and smelly.

When I'm skiing I wear the expo-weight long underwear, top and bottom, fleece shirt and jacket, shell jacket, hat, glove liners, mittens and over mitts. On my feet are sock liners, a thick plastic bag to trap vapor, heavy socks and boots. I stay plenty warm. At night, add a big down jacket, a raging fire. The first night I slept outside it was minus forty degrees F. We use an inner and outer sleeping bag, it's still cold. All you can think about is that when the sun rises you can start moving again and warm up.

Matt described some of the people in the group in his humorous way, said he hoped that the fish tank Bill was caring for was doing well, and signed off with, "Love, Matt. P.S. Brrr, brr, brrr."

In an undated letter sent a few weeks later he described the dogsledding in greater detail.

> Two nights ago, Thor, (my leader, a big Ukrainian man) and I took out a six-dog team for a late night run. When you hook up dogs, first you have to walk them to the tie-out from their houses. Since they love to run and pull, you have to lift their front legs off the ground or they'll drag you across the snow. If they get away from you they'll run away. If you've seen a husky run, they're real fast. Anyway, I put Tom's harness on and was hooking him to the wheel line of the sled, when I dropped the harness and he bolted. I ran after him down the road. Every 50 yards or so, I'd see the reflection of his eyes in my head lamp. I ran over a mile through the snow, following his tracks, worried that he'd be gone for good. Finally, I stopped to look for tracks… I heard Tom's collar jingling. He walked right up to me, kind of grinning but hanging his head low, and when he was 5 feet from me he turned and ran. I got up and talked to him. He weighs 120 pounds. I clipped his harness to my hammer loop on my pants. We ran back to the yard and went sledding.

Intense physical exertion and the cold beauty of the northland helped Matt regain his equilibrium and characteristic zest for life. In the past he had gravitated to other similar challenges. For his high school senior project he volunteered for two weeks to help with Rolf Peterson's seminal study of moose and wolf ecology on Lake Michigan's Isle Royal, the most remote of our national parks. This fifty-year effort is the longest continuous study of wild predator-prey interactions ever undertaken. Matt was not deterred by having to camp or cook meals on a one-burner stove in the snow in early March. His job was to hike the rugged, wild, and roadless terrain of the backcountry of the island in search of dead moose. When he found one, he performed a quick field autopsy, bagged the moose head, and then added it to his pack to transport back to headquarters for further study by the research team. Some of the heads with antlers weighed up to seventy-five pounds. The study was concerned with the causes of death—starvation or wolf kill. When I asked how he located the moose carcasses, Matt simply said, "Smell." Years later, his senior advisor told us that he continues to cite Matt's project to advisees as an example of a meaningful and challenging volunteer effort.

Matt sought challenges and pushed hard to learn his own limits. With this in mind, and in his memory, Luke thinks of a meaningful way to honor and remember him. And so here we are—Luke, Kathy, Bill, and I—driving southeast from Luke and Kathy's home in Jackson, Wyoming, on the anniversary of Matt's death.

It is sunny and warm for February. We head to Hoback Canyon and Iditarod Sled Dog Tours, a company advertising "always a howling good time." As we pull into the muddy parking lot we hear the din of the dogs—170 in all—and then see them nearby, a field of frenzied barking and leaping. A rope ties each dog to a large wooden spool, the sort used for winding cable. The dogs can enter the center of the spools for sleep or shelter, but this morning all of them are leaping wildly, straining at their ropes, yelping for breakfast or the freedom to run.

Amy, our high-spirited, redheaded leader, hands us heavy jackets and insulated boots, and teaches us some basics about the dogs and the sleds.

She explains that the dogs, who resemble small huskies, are bred to run and that they love nothing better. They possess the same spirit, strength, stamina, and speed as Eskimo work dogs, their ancestors and siblings. We will simply guide them as they run, pulling us behind. The litters have been named according to themes, such as Disney or Shakespearean characters, wildflowers, or state capitals. With her huge leather mitten, Amy points out the dogs in each team. My team includes Mickey, Daisy, and Polonius. She alerts us to the idiosyncrasies of certain dogs—one bites, another is lazy, and one runs to the left.

Although we lack experience, Amy seems confident that we are capable of this journey. She is right. She takes off in the lead sled, Luke and Kathy follow, and Bill and I take up the rear. The eight-dog teams run as fast as we allow, yapping constantly and furiously. Commands indicating "right" or "left" really work. Balancing on the sled's runner, one foot in front of the other, is challenging as the sled sways and swishes through the snow. I lean too far on one sharp curve and fall, rolling over and over in the snow, laughing and wondering how I will catch up. Bill manages to slow the dogs and I easily run up the slope and jump back on. Because Kathy is pregnant, she decides to ride seated on the sled with blankets bundled around her. She looks like a blonde Inuit princess.

Light snowfall sparkles as we head up Granite Creek Valley in the Bridger-Teton National Forest. In the distance around us rise the white, jagged peaks of the Gros Ventre Mountain Range. Straight, stately lodgepole pines, sub-alpine fir, and blue spruce border the trail. Along the creek stand groves of aspen and willow, and meadows of sagebrush, all frosted with snow.

Ten miles of sweeping and curving up the canyon. Cold wind in our faces. Whiteness all around. "Hi, Matt," I say. "Hi, Matt, out there somewhere."

We drive the sleds to a campsite tucked under a cliff beside Granite Creek Hot Springs. While the dogs rest, curled around each other and the tree trunks, we soak in the steaming, comforting springs. After a meal of trout cooked on a grill, we mount the sleds and snake down the valley over blue-shadowed snow. It is a day for Matt. It is a day to touch his soul.

Back home several days after this ride I feel myself sinking again. Pins and needles of anxiety shoot down my arms. I cry and cry. I cannot sleep. I have trouble doing mundane tasks. I have trouble doing anything. I cannot focus. I do not want to talk. I am not myself and I realize I need help. After struggling for a year I find that at this moment, on the anniversary of Matt's death, the wall I have built to hold myself together shatters into fragments. It falls away and I crumble into my grief and despair. I do not like taking medication for anything, but when I meet with a psychiatrist he looks at me and prescribes an antidepressant. Almost magically, in two days I feel the return of me. The profound sadness is still there, but I can function and be present in my life.

CHAPTER 19

Leaving Our Home

It's early summer of 2009. I turn the worn key in the familiar lock as I have done so many times these past thirty years. The startling, sharp smell of floor cleaner assaults me as I walk up the steps in the back hall. The kitchen is empty of our belongings and never before so clean. No cookbooks on the shelves, no table, no chairs, no magnets holding children's art on the refrigerator. The tile floor gleams. No stray sock, dog bone, or even a lost paper clip is in sight. On the countertop a realtor's glossy flyer lists rooms, baths, square footage, and assorted other facts that don't begin to tell the story of our house, but remind me it will not long be ours.

From the kitchen window I see the little, stone-rimmed pond we converted to a sandbox, then back to a pond. The pale green Solomon's seal I planted years ago droops over the water's surface, shaded by the huge silver maple. For a moment I think I see a group of small children playing on the grass, kicking a ball. Then taller children hoist a tepee they have just made to its full height, stand it firmly on the ground, and step back to admire their work. They stir mud in rubber buckets, smear it on each other, and shout with delight.

I see an evening past, late summer. On the deck that borders one side of the yard, we are toasting Matt and Elizabeth, his wife-to-be. Friends surround us. The bright floral cloths that Elizabeth and I painted cover the tables arranged around the yard. We laugh and talk and eat, stars overhead, the air warm and humid. The couple is young and beautiful. Love is all around them; surely they feel it. Candlelight glows on their faces as they sip champagne. I smile at this image in my mind's eye. Then the yard is still. I watch a few leaves spiral to the grass.

I look away and move quickly through the empty dining room, where beveled-glass windows shine little rainbows onto the dark wood floor. We celebrated the milestones of our lives around the orange table that is no longer here. I served a fancy breakfast at this table for Matt, his date, and friends early one Sunday, the morning after prom. The boys' faces were sweet and smooth above their tuxedos. The girls' sophisticated behavior quickly dissolved into giggles. The speeches, prayers, farewells, and toasts in honor of graduations, anniversaries, and birthdays—even the one hundredth birthday of the house—reverberate around me.

I walk quickly to the sunroom, which for years served as playroom for our boys and the neighborhood children. Their toys once blanketed the tile floor. I hear block towers tumbling, toy trucks zooming, and the body of a pink, rubber man clunking again and again as it hits the floor after floating down on a small parachute from the upstairs banister.

I can't imagine now that I ever approved it, but as a young teen Matt had several pet iguanas that lurked in the sunroom, hiding among the plants and preventing humans from enjoying this sun-filled space. The chameleons, which lived in a tank in his bedroom, were less intimidating. They ate live crickets he bought weekly with his allowance money. Every Saturday—feeding day—their chirps swelled in a hearty chorus heard throughout the second floor, diminishing to one or two feeble squeaks by Thursday.

At various ages, Matt loved and cared for dogs, turtles, gerbils, guinea pigs, and many species of fish. He managed to keep a crappie he caught on a lake in northern Wisconsin swimming happily in a tank for two years. Some of these creatures met unexpected ends, such as the desiccated chameleon we found on the bathroom floor at the base of the toilet, craning its nose upward as if looking for salvation. Others simply, quietly, made their escape. We captured some and joked that the others inhabited our dungeon-like basement, growing to enormous proportions.

The boys and their friends made creative use of our house, designating one dark and scary room in the basement the "Chemistry Lab," where they performed secret experiments. I never quite knew what they did there, but recently Matt's pal David wrote that in this small room lit by a single light bulb they mixed things together just to see what would happen. He noted that for some reason there were always lots of hard-boiled eggs in this secret space.

I remember screeching frantically to Matt from the front yard as he played his saxophone on the roof, three stories up. "What are you doing up there?" It strikes me as funny now, since it was obvious what he was doing. "Get down. Get down, right now!" Did he ignore me outright or could he really hear only "Summertime" as he leaned back, eyes shut, sending the steamy, sultry notes from his saxophone undulating out over the neighborhood?

I remember other sounds of our children: guitars and clarinets; remote-controlled cars careening through the front hall; the Grateful Dead, Phish, the Beastie Boys, and Bob Marley, as well as Beethoven and Bach, and Ravel's *Bolero* played at full volume. And, I remember, too, the quiet amidst disarray just after bedtime—replaced now by deeper quiet.

I tour the other empty rooms, each aching with memories joyful, sad, and poignant. Soon they will leak under the doors and float up the chimney, remaining only in our hearts. This house is an empty shell, the container that held us safe, a relic we no longer need. We already have moved into a new normal, into different lives, counting on our courage and memories—and some vague faith in our strength and resilience—to keep us going.

CHAPTER 20

Building the Shelter

THE WORK STARTS ON FRIDAY OF LABOR DAY WEEKEND 2009. THE DAY
is hot and sticky. Doug, a transplanted, so-called "Yooper"—a person
from the Upper Peninsula, or "UP" of Michigan—and volunteer actively
involved in creating and maintaining the North Country National Scenic
Trail in the Upper Peninsula, is the leader of our crew. Retired engineer,
geologist, educator, and former US Forest Service wilderness ranger, Doug
is also a hiker, backpacker, fisherman, cross-country skier, and a committed environmentalist. "He looks just like Jerry Garcia" (of the Grateful
Dead band), Luke and friend Micah say almost simultaneously. Burly and
gray-bearded, Doug wears a sweat-stained T-shirt; red suspenders stretch
over his belly to hold his jeans just below its bulk. He is a formidable
and untiring taskmaster to us volunteers, who consist of family, friends,
and kindly Yoopers with many helpful construction skills. Windmilling
his thick, muscular arms, Doug lumbers about, directing us here, hefting
something there. He wields a power saw, hunkers down to measure, and
then pounds in stakes. He talks and gestures incessantly, and succeeds in
carrying on two or three conversations at a time.

Doug handles the logistics of planning and building this shelter in Matt's memory. Early in the summer, Bill and Doug had stalked cross-country trails through the forest, searching for an appropriate site. They located a small rise on which the simple structure will face southeast with an expansive view of grassy wetlands, the nearby Sturgeon River, and giant white pine.

It will be an overnight resting place for hikers along the North Country Trail in Baraga County, Upper Michigan. The trail is rugged, spanning forty-six hundred miles from the shore of Lake Champlain and the Adirondack Mountains in New York to the plains of North Dakota, where it joins the Lewis and Clark National Historic Trail at the Missouri River.

Luke, Micah, Bill, friends, and energetic volunteers walk the half mile from the dirt road to the site lugging tools, a generator, and twelve-foot-long lengths of rough-sawn board. They traverse the rocky, mossy trail through the woods, and balance on a newly built boardwalk through a cedar swamp. The first day Luke and Micah each walk seventeen miles lugging armloads of boards from the dirt road where a truck dropped off the lumber. The next day they log twenty-one miles, sweating out their grief as they tramp from road to river, then river to road.

The work is hot and strenuous, but the men quickly frame out the structure, a sturdy, geometric skeleton of hemlock. Watching them struggle and sweat, I remember how Matt embraced the age-old phrase "Nothing worth doing is ever easy."

Micah, a friend since childhood to both Luke and Matt, was often part of our family's activities. He is married now and has a young daughter. Some months after working on the shelter, he wrote to me about the project.

> It was hot and sweaty but so satisfying and cathartic as well. The pile looked impossibly big to begin with and never seemed to shrink until suddenly I was estimating how few

trips were left. Reminds me of children growing—when you are in the presence of them you are not really noticing until one day you turn around and they are practically five feet tall. I felt close to Luke carrying that lumber in. We have a bond that will always be there. It felt good to do that work with him. It was a metaphor for sharing his burden of the loss of Matt in a physical way. There was lots of time to reflect on all those hikes in and out. When spending time with your family, I find myself thinking of what Matt might be saying or doing. While Luke would dive right in to a challenge, such as the wood carrying, I could hear Matt making some wisecracks about it and maybe grumbling in a good-natured way, raising the ire of Luke, and then rising to the challenge and working just as hard or harder than anyone.

The shelter is nearly finished that weekend. It is a simple nine-by-twelve-foot structure with three closed walls built of board-and-batten hemlock siding. The screened-in front keeps the space almost bug-free. Inside are two sets of wood bunks, pegs for hanging packs, and a rustic shelf to hold a metal box protecting the journal. I imagine hikers who spend the night here writing comments such as "Great hike today. Mosquitoes biting and flies attacking, but the beauty of the woods is worth it." Or, "Heard wolves howling after the rain last night, but we were safe and dry."

Matt always seemed at home and in love with nature. At age ten, with a little YMCA camping experience behind him, he decided one summer evening just before sunset to camp alone in the woods near our home. I tried to dissuade him, but decided that no harm would come to him and, wanting to respect his adventuresome spirit, allowed him to go. (I am not sure how I would have stopped him.) He took a small green tent, his sleeping bag, and a flashlight, and marched determinedly off into the woods. Luke and I were a bit concerned but also certain he would return in an hour or two when the sun had fully set. Eleven o'clock came, then twelve. No Matt. I suddenly awoke at about six in the morning, still dressed. Where was Matt? I woke Luke and we hurried into the woods. After walking some distance we spotted the peak of the little tent a short way off the path, ringed by maple trees, morning sun dappling the ground. Still frightened, I approached the tent and lifted the flap. There he was, curled on top of the sleeping bag, safe, sound, and peacefully asleep.

CHAPTER 21

The Fountain

THE STATELY BRICK CHURCH WHERE MATT AND ELIZABETH WERE MARRIED
and where we held Matt's farewell service stands along a wooded road
north of Milwaukee. Church officials had planned to erect a drinking
fountain for the convenience of the many runners, bikers, and walkers
who pass by, and now agree to build it in memory of Matthew. The fountain will stand at the southeast corner of the church, next to a labyrinth
and easily accessible to all.

With the family's assistance I designed a simple fountain in the shape
of a vertical, slightly spiraling rectangle just high enough to be convenient
for a biker to drink from. Two polished sides of flecked, gray granite join
a rough-hewn surface. The fourth side is lined with craggy, vertical ridges
running from basin to ground. On one of the smooth surfaces "Remembering Matthew Manger-Lynch" is inscribed.

Late on the Sunday afternoon of September 27, 2009, the day before
what would have been Matt's thirtieth birthday, we commemorate the
fountain. Again, Scott, our counselor and the priest who conducted both
Matt's wedding and funeral, assists us.

At the center of the grass labyrinth, Scott places a ceramic bowl. To the strains of Handel's *Water Music* coming from Scott's boom box we step one by one along the path of the labyrinth to its center, each holding green-and-yellow Green Bay Packer (Matt was a great fan!) mugs filled with water from the fountain. We pour water from mug to bowl, then follow the path out to wait at the fountain. Scott, who has walked behind us with the bowl, hoists it above our heads; with a brief prayer of remembrance he tips the contents into the basin of the fountain. The healing water overflows the shiny brim to slide down the jagged surface into the earth. Luke staggers away, wiping his eyes, overcome by sadness. Elizabeth pulls from her purse a bottle of Matt's favorite champagne, pops the cork, and pours the champagne into the fountain. "This is for you, Babe," she says. We all laugh, then cry.

Later we have dinner at the familiar table where Matt had melded into Elizabeth's family, experiencing Jane's hospitality, and sharing great food that he and his father-in-law, Bob, had prepared. We talk small talk, mostly, but now and then a memory of Matt bursts into the conversation— "Remember when?" We eat and drink and he is with us.

CHAPTER 22

Journey Not Chosen

AFTER MATT'S DEATH, A STREAM OF CARDS AND HEARTFELT LETTERS FLOWS into our mailbox. One day our friendly mailman asks me if we are celebrating a special anniversary. I tell him no. I write thank-you letters to everyone. Each letter is both a sacred act and a distraction.

The flowers and plants in every room wilt and die. I toss them out, crying with each armful. In the midst of the empty vases and baskets, Bill and I face each other in despair.

"How are we going to do this?" I ask him.

"We are doing it," he answers.

We take long walks in March and April. No matter where we go, we are raw and cold. Choosing a different park or woods every day, we keep moving, keep walking—one foot, then the next foot. The snow melts, the wildflowers begin to appear, and we keep walking.

"How are we supposed to do this?" I keep asking Bill.

"We are doing it," he says, again and again.

We continue to consider the questions that hang in the air around us even when we are not giving them voice. Why? How could . . . ? Why Matt?

Why us? There are no logical answers.

I do not want answers to the questions I have about the driver who hit Matt. Did he see Matt coming? Did he try to slow down? Did he resent the presence of a biker on the road? Is he distraught over killing Matt? Does he think about that moment? In that moment, the worst happened. There is nothing good to be mined from this vein of thought.

Friends try to help, and do, by providing meals or walking with me. Of course, no one knows what to say, but I appreciate the attempts. I meet two mothers who also have lost adult children recently in sudden accidents. Our talks over lunch or coffee are meaningful and teary. We know each other's sorrow, but wish otherwise. One of the most helpful and simple comments from a neighbor rings true: "You just have to keep going." And we do.

Still, nothing really helps. Our talks with Scott come close. He leads us gently on this unchosen journey. At first, we see him weekly. We walk as if in a trance—one foot, then the next—down the bland hallway past the dentist's and urologist's offices. Once in Scott's waiting room, we sit beside a stack of dated magazines before sinking, at last, into the comfort of his office sofa.

Scott encourages us and offers perspectives that are at least thought provoking, at best affirming and enlightening. And he offers a place where we can cry.

"It is an honor to walk with you in your grief," he says at the end of several appointments. During another session, Scott says, "I think you are doing just great." I recoil and feel anger surging in my cheeks. My palms start sweating. "Great?" I say. "We're miserable."

"I know," he says. "You're feeling exactly what you need to be feeling. You are feeling your grief. Many people cannot do that."

Scott's description of grief reflects my own experience. He says that at the start it is as if you are standing with your back to the ocean. The waves of grief striking you are constant, relentless, raging, pummeling, leveling, and bring you to your knees. Gradually, the waves roll in less often. You are overcome less frequently. Longer and longer interludes between the slapping waves allow you to stay vertical, to breathe, even to laugh.

Scott is right. As time passes, the waves come only now and again, but still they come, and unexpectedly. With each, I struggle to keep my footing, to hold my balance in the face of this great, drowning force. Sometimes I lose my equilibrium and sink, nearly dissolving into the waves. But each time I manage to surface and step onto firm ground once again. We are doing it.

CHAPTER 23

Other Markers, Not Stones

MANY ACTS OF KINDNESS COME IN THE WAKE OF MATT'S DEATH. IN NEW York on the day after the accident, a high school friend of Matt's brings an orchid to La Grenouille, asking to place it in the kitchen. A friend in Hawaii tosses a lei of *plumeria* into the ocean and sends us a photo of the pink blossoms floating on shimmering, turquoise waves.

Matt's in-laws fund a chef to work with cooks to improve meals for families at the Working Boys' Center in Quito, Ecuador. Elizabeth writes in the center's newsletter: "Matthew had many wonderful opportunities in his career as a chef, but he wouldn't have had them without his commitment to work, his need to constantly learn new things, his reverence for the natural world, and a healthy sense of adventure. It seems that Matthew shared the values that we promote here."

The director of the Mwangaza Education Center in Arusha, Tanzania, plants an evergreen tree, an *araucaria*, in memory of Matt, who had climbed nearby Mount Kilimanjaro with Bill and me when he was about twenty years old. Several years later, while Matt was in college, Bill and I volunteered at the center in Arusha, the city that had served as the starting point for our trek. A photo we receive shows the tree standing just inside the gate to the grounds in an open, grassy area, and although in a distant corner of the world, its branches seem to reach slightly toward us in a healing gesture.

In Oslo, Elin, a foreign exchange student who lived with us for a year and considered Matt her brother, mourns him. And closer to home, many donate to the YMCA summer camp where Matt was both camper and counselor. We are heartened by this caring kindness and remembering.

We sponsor a park bench for the neighborhood park where Matt and Luke played as children. The bench backs up to a ravine where they rode their dirt bikes with pals; it faces a grassy spot where we once held birthday parties, and the tennis court where he and Elizabeth played. The plaque on the bench's backrest displays Matt's name, dates, and a quote from William Wordsworth.

My heart leaps up
when I behold
A rainbow in the sky.

CHAPTER 24

Life Continues

LUKE AND KATHY NOW HAVE A BABY NAMED MAX. AT THE AGE OF thirty-five, Luke is thoroughly occupied with the needs of baby, family, and work. I wonder if he ever thinks of his own parents raising him and Matt. I am certain he recognizes now how much a parent gives to a baby, to a child. He may understand all that we have lost in Matt, but his loss is distinctly his own. Since his birth, he and Matt were good pals. Of course, occasional bickering and rivalries arose, but the quarrels and squabbles were usually quickly resolved. Luke exerted the power and privilege of the firstborn; that is, until Matt's height exceeded his by several inches, a shift in size that brought about equilibrium. They treasured their brotherhood and their friendship.

Now Luke's brother and best friend are gone. The only person who shared his childhood history, gone. His snowboarding, cooking, camping, fishing buddy, gone. The only uncle of his child, a piece of his future, someone who might have shared the burden of his elderly parents, gone.

Bill and I have continued to walk. We find it soothing. In early April 2010, on an overcast, chilly day, we walk in the Kettle Moraine—a hilly, unglaciated part of Wisconsin west of Milwaukee. We have done this many springs to catch sight of the returning sandhill cranes. We absentmindedly choose a trail that leads us out of the green, spring woods into a recently burned area. This gray expanse of jagged, black trees and charcoal stumps is desolate, and I don't know why, but we continue to walk on the dirt path leading us through the ashes. We have come too far to go back. I think about the new growth that will eventually emerge from the darkness here, wondering how it will manage.

Then we hear the throaty sound. Two sandhill cranes fly overhead searching for nesting spots, croaking and cackling their presence, greeting spring's arrival and announcing their own. They do not land, but persist in their circling and searching.

Later that year, on a Sunday in mid-July, I find myself in the dank basement of our new condo. I extract a big, flat basket from a jumble of others I had wedged into a corner when we moved here. It is the perfect size. As I unwind green satin ribbon from the arched handle, I realize that the basket originally held a huge arrangement of forsythia sent by La Grenouille for Matt's service. I have neither the time nor the fortitude to ponder the sad irony of this. I keep unwinding, and attach a new, pink ribbon.

The basket will hold gifts for a baby girl Elizabeth and her partner, Nathan, the baby's father, will call Summer. They are joyful as they await her birth, hoping she will be born before fall arrives. The baby shower that Alison and I are hosting for Elizabeth begins in several hours. We still have things to do: arrange the table, ice the champagne. I am excited about the soon-to-be-born infant. I expect the baby will bring happiness to Elizabeth, give her hope and a changed outlook on her future. This is not what she planned for her life. Neither is it what I anticipated. My connection to the baby will be distant, but still, I am happy for Elizabeth and Nathan.

In August the baby is born, healthy and beautiful, but later than expected. I think she liked it where she was—less complicated, more familiar. The photos show her to be a lovely baby with that "having come from afar" look of newborns.

On September 3, 2010, Elizabeth sends an e-mail.

> Hi Barbara,
>
> Nice to hear from you. I have been thinking about you because I have sensed that you are feeling not great, lately.
>
> As I become a parent more and more each day, I think about what it is to have a child, and well . . . it makes the idea of losing a child so much more powerful. Though I have said this before, I say it with a new understanding: I am so sorry for your loss. And, I am sorry that you are right now having to make your way through some not-so-great-feelings. I, too, have been feeling a little weepy lately.
>
> It is September and it is Matt's birthday this month. And it is almost Packer season! (Side note: we have been doing little "follow the Packer booties" vision games with Summer with the booties you sent her.) I think seeing the first cyclists in the springtime and then Packer season are two seasons when Matt is really on my mind.
>
> It is odd (or maybe not) that we all have been feeling low lately. (Low? The only word I have to describe it.) Must be something in the air—definitely, it's the time of year—or perhaps something that our brains aren't meant to make sense of. As Matt was fond of saying, "There are more things in heaven and earth, Horatio, than are dreamt of in your philosophy." (It's from *Hamlet*.)
>
> I love you both and you mean a lot to me. I will call you when I can—today or tomorrow. Would be nice to chat.
>
> Elizabeth

CHAPTER 25

What Remains

IN OUR OLD HOUSE, MATT HAD LONG AGO ABANDONED HIS CHILDHOOD toys. Our cupboards were full of his youth: little troll dolls, a beanbag reindeer family, Matchbox cars and trucks, math medals, his saxophone and folders of sheet music marked by both Matt and his teacher, medals from state music contests, baseball cards, a small, light blue soccer sock, worn-out hiking boots, fishing rods, backpacks.

I remember finding a commendation from a favorite high school teacher, which I placed in a small plastic frame. He wrote, "By getting a 99.3% on the recent Bonding and Phases test, Matt has revealed an unusually high level understanding of skills and ideas in College Chemistry. It was a pleasure to grade such a unique paper and realize that Matt developed such a fine comprehension." I remember Matt shrugging this off, but with a slight smile.

I find as well his read-with-delight collection of Calvin and Hobbs books and several copies of his beloved *Lord of the Rings,* and a name badge from the camp where he was both a camper and counselor. These are the remnants of a boy's life—the precious treasures of a mother.

Also left behind is Matt's adult home where he lived with Elizabeth. A few days after his death, I happened to see his biking shoes there in a basket by the stairs, and several shirts on the floor of the laundry room where he had tossed them. He left behind his white chef coats, a wine collection, his car, bikes, and tools. In the basement were the hams, prosciutto, and sausages—the charcuterie that he had hung there to cure.

Elizabeth is a skilled photographer, so our family has many images of Matt as a handsome young man taken during their five-year marriage. I frame and hang several that are especially meaningful. One shows a vast expanse of blue Green Bay at its summer best. Tiny, in the distance, a shirtless Matt paddles a red kayak away from us toward a hazy horizon. In another, tanned, wearing a billed cap, and gazing away from us, he leans on an old boat. Elizabeth took many others—close-ups of Matt's hands working with food in countless ways, a shot from the rear as he flexes his muscles before attacking a clogged drain with a plumbing gadget, and Matt concentrating intensely as he untangles a fishing line or smiling delightedly as he raises a freshly caught bass for the camera. I am able to smile at some as I remember his boisterous personality. Others send waves of nausea, blades of sorrow, or recurring waves of grief pulsing through me. How much of life he will miss. How much we miss him.

Elizabeth compiles a beautifully designed, heartfelt book of her photographs and Matt's recipes in a tribute titled, *Cooking and Eating with Matt.* The cover photo focuses closely on his left hand holding a plump tomato as he punctures its taut skin with the tip of his knife blade. Glossy, red borders frame more photos of his hands deftly cutting zucchini into julienne slivers. In another, he arranges a tiny slice of salmon, a circle of sour cream, and a dot of black caviar on a homemade cracker. The recipes, ranging from Spaghetti with Clams and Red Sauce to *Gougére* with Blue

Cheese and Pear, are not difficult to prepare, but Elizabeth's accompanying reminiscences are piercing to read.

> Matt loved to cook and eat. Simply put, food excited him and cooking was his creative outlet. This book is my attempt at passing along Matt's culinary passion and talents, which he so readily shared with others.
>
> Although Matt was very disciplined in the kitchen, he did not have a lot of strict rules when it came to food and eating. His clothes were often food spattered and he didn't care which fork to use—only that what was on the end of the fork was really, really tasty.
>
> Meat and all things pork were some of Matt's favorite foods. He butchered his own pigs, smoked his own bacon in the backyard, and taught himself the art and craft of drying and curing meats. He liked bacon on pretty much everything. His favorite burger from Kuma's Corner in Chicago, named the Led Zeppelin, included ten ounces of beef topped with pulled pork, bacon, cheddar cheese, and pickles. Matt's plan had been to open a small restaurant serving wine, his own charcuterie, and cheeses.

Elizabeth's book includes a number of photos of the glistening, pink meats and fat-streaked sausages Matt had made, including duck sausage with pale green pistachios, pancetta, and roast pig. Under a recipe for spiced almonds, she notes Matt's *other* favorite snacks, which he claimed to eat only on road trips. The evidence: bright wrappers from White Cheddar Cheezits and Original Combos (cheese-filled pretzels) cluttering the car floor. "Totally grease bombs," Elizabeth writes.

The last two pages present, on the left, a grouping of photos of Matt's notebooks—full of busy lists of ingredients, jottings, and ideas for dishes such as saffron mussel risotto, sweet and sour turnip, herb spaetzle, veal piccata, and *sauce moutarde*. The photograph on the right page, the last in her book, displays Matt's largest notebook, spread open to a page on which he wrote the heading "Career Plan" and the subcategories of "When," "Where," and "Why."

To me, his mom, Matt gave cooking tips and recipes to cherish. Most he did not write down, but relayed quickly over the phone or in a brief e-mail. He became impatient when I asked, "Well, Matt, just *how big* a handful?" or "*How long* will this take to make?" His recipes remind me somewhat of my grandmother's. They both used directions such as "cook until done" or "bake until ready," but Matt's include many ingredients she likely wouldn't have recognized, and processes and outcomes that are more complex. I can imagine her raised eyebrows at Butternut Squash Wallet on Raisin Bread Toast with Candied Walnuts and Onion Sauce, a delectable, mouth-watering, nickel-sized appetizer requiring ten pistils of saffron as well as considerable skill and time.

My favorite recipe, Compote Navidad, which Matt wrote down at my insistence, I prepare during the holidays. The Christmas season following his death, Elizabeth, Bill, Luke, and I send cards with Elizabeth's photograph of this appetizer arranged on a wooden platter surrounded by pine branches in a candle's glow. The card includes the recipe, which, characteristic of Matt's cooking style, calls for a burst of wintery spices.

I serve this whenever the occasion seems right, and smile and cry as I measure with a wine bottle.

Seeking to preserve the directions for other favorite dishes, Luke assembles the recipes Matt had given him, and requests others from Matt's friends, including college classmates. In the section of Luke's collection titled "Tidbits," I enjoy reading one from Siri, which—like many of these recipes—dates from the days before Matt's education at Le Cordon Bleu.

Compote Navidad, A Christmas Chutney

Bring to a rolling boil for ten minutes the following ingredients:

1 bottle red wine

1 wine bottle of water

2/3 wine bottle of sugar

4 drops Tabasco

Put all of these in a tea ball or muslin bag:

2 tablespoons peppercorns   2 tablespoons coriander seeds

1/4 small cinnamon stick   1 tablespoon whole cloves

10 whole allspice berries

Then add:

2 cups dried figs cut in thirds

2 cups dried apricots cut in thirds

Boil for 15 minutes.

Then add:

4 pears peeled and cut into 3/4 inch cubes

3 apples peeled and cut into cubes

Cook until almost dry—about 1 hour and 45 minutes.

Serve over goat cheese with crackers or bread.

"Imagine a nice, cold vodka martini with dried Tang dripping down the rim of the glass—a throwback to Matt's Midwest roots," she writes. "He always made great food that had a sense of humor."

Masami, a favorite friend, contributes this: "PEANUT BUTTER. I just remember Matt putting peanut butter in everything, usually mean marinades with soy sauce, and mirin. And also in smoothies that always came out a weird beige-brown color."

Another friend recalls, "Matt almost assassinated a group of Macalester students during one of his early kitchen concoctions. We were sitting in my living room when Matt disappeared. Within minutes acrid smoke began belching from the kitchen. I arose from our lollygagging only to find him searing—What?—Jalapeno peppers!"

And, from Matt's best friend, Nick: Matt's Famous Basic Spice-Mulled Cider Recipe. "To a jug of cider," writes Nick, "add star anise, three to four cardamom pods, a cinnamon stick, three to four whole cloves, and nutmeg. Heat thoroughly over low heat. Add a shot of whiskey/bourbon—whichever you prefer or have around—to mug, and pour cider over. Repeat as needed. That's it! Enjoy."

Lastly, Elizabeth offers what she says may have been Matt's most favorite cooking tip: "Add bacon."

I remember that in quieter moments we often prepared what Matt and Luke called "Mom's Dutch Oven Potatoes"—not really a recipe, but a favorite outdoor dish baked in a cast-iron dutch oven. Luke's recollection of how the preparation typically evolved brings back memories.

> We would be hanging around the cabin and my mom and Matt would start slicing potatoes and grating cheese. Matt would say something like, "Well, don't you have any gruyere?" or "It needs *way* more butter than that."

Eventually, Matt would get distracted and join Dad and me as we snuck out to go fishing. My mom would stoke up a fire in the fire pit and watch over these potatoes until well after dark, hoping Matt, Dad, and I would come in from fishing and eat dinner.

Ingredients: sliced baking potatoes, Vidalia or sweet onions, blue cheese, white cheddar cheese, Parmesan cheese. Butter the dutch oven. Slice a stick of butter into pats and add a cup or two of half-and-half. Layer all the ingredients except the Parmesan. Lots of salt and pepper as you go. Put Parm on top last. Put dutch oven on low coals. Top dutch oven with more coals. Cook till done. Mmmm.

Luke says that Matt had an uncanny ability to make complex cooking simple. He could immediately describe three creative ways to cook the precious bag of morel mushrooms you had gathered, how to smoke trout or whitefish in several easy steps, or unlikely steps to take to make asparagus taste especially great using only a few ingredients. On his last Christmas, Matt gave us a paella pan and one of the few recipes he committed to paper, Christmas Paella. In addition to the directions for preparing the shrimp, clams, mussels, and chicken, he added a time-saving tip: "Invite friends who don't mind picking out bones and shells." Matt had many friends who didn't mind.

When our family and friends prepared Christmas dinner in Luke and Kathy's kitchen a few years ago, everyone took on a task, whether capable or not. We ate appetizers Matt and Luke produced while we cooked: pear, caramelized onion, and blue cheese on puff pastry; and *escalantes,* bacon wrapped around Medjool dates stuffed with goat cheese. Luke and Matt, both skilled grillers, smoked a brined turkey on the grill. Whenever they slid the deck door to check its state of doneness, rich smells drifted in.

Matt ricocheted around the kitchen from one pan or dish to another, a whirlwind slamming down pan lids, improvising tools, expertly and rapidly slicing, dicing, sautéing, flipping, stirring, tasting. The crashing and banging and his outbursts of laughter were sound effects integral to his style, part of his rhythm, intensity, and joy as he created. He offered gentle supervision to my amateur gravy making. "Mom, do you know there's a way to do this without getting those lumps?" he asked, gentle and humorous teacher that he was.

In the end, a great dinner appeared—a meal cooked with wine and laughter, and love, the most delicious ingredient of all.

CHAPTER 26

What Else Can We Do?

WHAT ELSE CAN WE DO? WE HOPE MATT WILL WALK BY THE STONE AT the campsite in Michigan and stop there to take in the view. We hope he will rest in the shelter on the North Country Trail, and hear the slap of beavers' tails and birdsong. We hope he will pass the fountain near the church, and will notice the bench that bears his name in the park where he played as a child.

As I reflect on these memories of Matt and the ways our family has tried to honor him, I recognize that the ceremonies and dedications have been as much for us as for him. We are yearning to hold on to him, to create something solid and tangible in his place. Still, no stone can fill the void in our lives. All we can do is hope that Matt has an awareness of us. Hope that he knows of our love for him. Hope that he has knowing beyond our own.

The constant swirl of memory of Matt's birth and childhood, of his manhood, and then of his death to this world, I hold close. This is what I do not want to lose. I watch his widow continue her life with another gentle young man. I watch Matt's friends build lives that no longer include him— watch as their wounds from his absence heal.

I watch as his brother struggles, and with great resolve and courage continues his life. As Luke and Kathy create a family, he feels the return of joy. The birth of their baby, Max, born small and premature but healthy, shines a strong little beam that pierces the gray armor of grief I wear. I remember what it is to fall in love with a baby, what it is to hold in my arms a new and tiny life. His needs and cries nudge all of us into the present. I consider his vulnerability more intensely than I did that of my own babies. I hope for his health and welfare.

The expression "having a hole in your heart" does not pertain to me. I do not have a hole. I harbor within me a stone. I imagine that it is a jagged piece of white limestone, perhaps severed from Matt's stone but heavier. It lodges near my heart where I carried Matt before his birth to this world. It weighs me down. When I am quiet and alone it is the most painful. There are times it twists and slices me with its sharp edges.

When I catch sight of a fit, young man riding a bike and think for an instant that it could be Matt, I feel an aching stab. When I talk with a friend who cannot bring herself to mention Matt's name or perhaps has forgotten him entirely, I feel miserable. When I see a photo of a handsome, smiling chef displaying a new dish, I hurt. When I listen to one of his voice messages, still saved, and hear his strong, bright voice—"Hi, folks. It's Matt. I'm back. Had a good trip. Hope all is well. Talk to you soon."—I am taken aback. When I hold baby Max's tiny hand, and remember he has neither uncle nor cousins, the stone twists again.

In recent days, the jagged stone nudges itself into a safe corner, perhaps just under my heart where I barely sense its presence, but it remains a dead and heavy weight. I will carry it with me to the end of my own days.

CHAPTER 27

This Is Not Going Away

INTERTWINED WITHIN THE ORDINARY EVENTS OF AN ORDINARY DAY, I AM reminded of the loss of Matt in unexpected, often shocking ways that upset the equilibrium I struggle to maintain. Memories float through my awareness, rising unexpectedly, bringing out goose bumps, a smile, or an ache that plunges deeply. Reminders of him hover about. Because I do not have him near me, my present thoughts of him sway and wander, intermingling between the distant and not-so-distant past. I see him as an infant—a moment later, as a tall, young man. As Luke says, "This is not going to go away."

A recent voice message from a neighbor leaves me in tears.

> I called because I saw a new bench in the park and walked over to see it. There was Matt's name. Matt was indeed a person whose heart leapt up when he saw a rainbow. He was an artistic, sensitive, sweet young man. Of all my son's friends, Matt was my favorite. He'd see me in the yard, stop by, and call out, "Hi, Mr. D." He came in to have a glass of wine with me when my son wasn't home. I really, really liked him.

> Dylan + Alison
> My heart leapt enthusiastically when I opened your gift. I immediately removed my shorts to try yours on and haven't removed them since. 12 days of Christmas? No, 12 days wearing these amazing boxer shorts more like it. From now on I'll remember the 25th of December no longer as Jesus' birth, but as the day I got these boxers. Woohoo
> Matt

This year on February 24, my nephew Dylan and his wife (our friend Alison) e-mail a scanned copy of a thank-you note Matt had sent them for their gift of mistletoe boxer shorts several years ago. His familiar handwriting on my computer screen causes me to gasp.

A friend reminds me that in her family they often repeated a remark Matt made at the age of seven. The school bus driver had reprimanded him for something naughty and when I confronted him he said, "Mother, I am not a perfect boy." Throughout the years, her family repeated this phrase when one or another of them did something out of line. I remember that no, he was not a perfect boy.

Matt's childhood friend David writes to me. He recalls the time when they were five years old and went without permission to the neighborhood store. They spent all their money on candy. Delighting in this accomplishment and their independence, they tossed the bag of treats up in the air only to have the precious cache snag in the branches of the big silver maple in our yard. There it hung, far out of their reach. It probably would have been devoured by squirrels if Bill hadn't rescued it for them.

On a long drive one weekend, Bill comes to tears as he reminisces about the coral reef tank project that Matt, inspired by the marine biology course he had just completed, coaxed him to take on. "Dad, all you do is work and go to meetings," Matt had said. "You need a hobby." Of course, Matt would not be around to help maintain the coral reef tank, a complex step up from an earlier, freshwater tank.

Cleaning and care of the fifty-five gallon tank became part of Dad's morning ritual. Changing water, checking salinity, adding chemicals—calcium chloride, strontium, iodine, and molybdenum—in exact proportions were crucial to keep the pagoda, flat corals, open brain corals, and others alive. The battle with algae that threatened to overcome the tank became more than a hobby. Matt's regular calls home, first from college then later from New York, Paris, and Chicago, always began with, "What's happening with the corals?" followed by a specific question or two about Chompy, the slim, golden tang fish, or whether or not the new snails were keeping the tank clean. Bill's maintenance was nearly perfect except for a few major overflows onto the old playroom floor. He did this for ten years, including the two following Matt's death, faithful in his commitment not just to these mysterious, silent creatures, but also to the memory of their shared endeavor. Bill did not want to break that bond. However, without the calls, support, interest, and encouragement from Matt, his own interest diminished, his vigilance too lonely a task. When we moved to our new house, Bill donated the corals, the fish, and their tank to a local aquarium.

Although I did not share in this project, I did enjoy sitting on the old wicker couch, soothed by the waving arms of coral—magenta, lime green, violet. I still can see Bill and Matt standing silhouetted against the greenish glow of the tank as they hold up a vial to test for a vital ingredient, father and son absorbed in their effort and in each other.

Rustling through my desk for stamps, I find a sheet of labels that Matt designed for the beer that he and Bill produced—another hobby initiated by Matt. The label shows an image of our dog and the brand name, "Mad Corgi Brew—Same Great Brew since 1997."

Taking great fun in measuring and boiling, they created scotch ales, porters, and belgian chimays, many bottles of which traveled back to college with Matt. I fold the labels and carefully slide them back into a cubbyhole of the desk not knowing if Bill will use them again.

People's comments, less frequent now, also astound me. I see a friend who asks, "How are you doing?" The question is casual, but I reply, "It's up and down." "Still?" she asks, surprised. Yes, still. This is not going away.

CHAPTER 28

Riding Through Grief

BILL, LUKE—HIS THREE-YEAR-OLD SON, MAX, RIDING HIS SHOULDERS—
and I return to the woods in the Upper Peninsula in June 2011, more than
three years after Matt's death. We walk in silence on the North Country
Trail, crossing the bog on the wooden walkway on the way to the shelter,
then onto the path, where layers of pine needles soften the rocky forest
floor. Golden mid-day sunlight makes its way to the sepia-toned ground,
creating crisscross shadow patterns of branches and leaves.

"There's the tree I always look for," Luke says, pointing to a birch growing out of a dead and weathered stump. Its healthy roots encircle the gray
stump, twining around it as they reach for nourishment from the ground
below. I had never noticed it among the abundant plant life. Spritely ferns,
sarsaparilla, and delicate lady slippers have sprung up, as has a small cluster of *Monotropa uniflora*, also called Indian pipe, corpse flower, or ghost
flower. Lacking chlorophyll, the ghost flower has a bluish, waxy look and
glows white in the cool shade. I wonder at the fact that it grows close to the
place where we want to honor Matt's life.

At the shelter, we face the calm Sturgeon River. Insects hum gently above us. I feel the soothing touch of this place, of nature's unrelenting cycle of growth, death, decay, and new growth.

In front of the shelter, a chunk of timber provides a riverside seat, shaded by four slim cedars. There are four, like our original family. A fifth dead cedar lists at an angle to the right, a reminder of what has befallen us.

I look out over the river hoping to see a moose wading through the marshland, but all is quiet. Across the river, a slim line of shore divides the density of the forest from its exact reflection in the dark river. Another forest appears to lie below the surface, a facsimile world beneath the one we call real. The mirage-like shimmer lures my imagination, invites me to believe in a world beyond the one I know, a world where Matt might be, a world unknown to us who exist above this flat surface. I like to think it is just out of our reach, but there, beneath the surface of our knowing. The reassuring reflection is heartening, mysterious. Matt is there, not with us, but there. This thought is uplifting. It is within the realm of my reality. A slight breeze wobbles, then blurs, the world of reflection.

I am reminded of a dream Elizabeth shared with me. In her dream Matt said to her, "I'm OK, don't worry. It's kind of boring, but I'm happy."

I think that if Matt were here he might tromp out through the grass into the river to see how deep this section of the Sturgeon is. "Hey, guys! Look how deep! Come on out!" Or he might try to find a big turtle or search for the beaver that felled a pile of trees just behind the shelter.

The shelter is reassuring. Matt would love to sleep here. The volunteers who recently finished installing the skylights also swept clean the wide floorboards. The small structure stands firm, still smelling of fresh-sawn wood. We place a bottle of whisky for weary travelers beside the journal, and after boosting little Max to an upper bunk, sit for a moment in silence.

We feel welcome, as any hiker will. The place is peaceful, the shelter simple but comfortable. I pick up the journal and read the few entries, the last written by our friend Jim.

> *We ate lunch in the shelter. Beautiful day, sunny but cold. Heard the geese on a neighboring lake.*

> *Gorgeous day. Close to 60 degrees and sunny! I've spent several nights here. Wonderful place.*

> *Walking the trail with Bill, and remembering Matt. Fine man whose love of nature will be honored here.*

I want to stay and weep, but I am beyond weeping. Most of my sadness I have stuffed down or used up or hidden in false cheerfulness.

Later, I walk alone around the lake, and climb the hill to the site of Matt's stone. The arbor, offering entry to this spirit-filled space, still stands, having lasted through two harsh winters. Tendrils of fishing line, which originally bound ferns and daisies, still dangle from the intersections of the arbor's slim branches. The only sound is the movement of the white pines high above. The stone looks fresh and still bright white. I kneel and with a leaf wipe off a small bird stain. I lightly touch Matt's footprints and run my hands down the carving, part smooth, part roughly textured. I brush away the dried pine needles piled near the front of the stone to reveal the words "Here is my dream home." It was. It is.

Epilogue

ON A SATURDAY MORNING, I PERCH ON A STATIONARY BIKE IN A SPIN CLASS, tuning out the music and the instructor's shrill voice. My spot near the windows offers a view of the gray, drizzly day. Through the mist outside I see a lime-green slash, the roof of a gas station flanked by a Chinese restaurant. Directly across the street an occasional passerby appears. A couple with a shopping bag walks a big, white dog; a petite woman with a turquoise umbrella hurries in the opposite direction. Then a small boy on a large bicycle whizzes by. I wonder absently about these people and their stories as they pass a blooming tulip tree, a forsythia bush working to bud, and an American flag hanging limply in the wetness.

I suddenly realize that the backdrop for this scene is the brick wall and big garage doors of a funeral home. I look away as the instructor in the class gives a riding tip, and when I look back notice that one of the big doors has opened. Nothing enters nor exits; nothing is visible but blackness. Still, I watch the gaping dark maw, expectantly.

I hear the instructor encourage the class with a scream. "Keep going. Keep going. You can do it." And, I do. I am doing better than a year ago, and better than the spring before that.

About the Author

Barbara Manger is an author, artist, and art educator. Her first book, the award-winning *Mary Nohl: Inside and Outside, A Biography of the Artist*, was published by the Greater Milwaukee Foundation in 2010. Manger also co-authored a young person's version of the book, *Mary Nohl: A Lifetime in Art*, published by the Wisconsin Historical Society in 2013.

Photo courtesy of Elizabeth G. Lynch.

Manger has taught at Cardinal Stritch University and Alverno College. Her artwork has been exhibited nationally, and her prints and drawings are included in a number of public and private collections. She has served on the boards of numerous non-profit organizations, including the Board of Trustees of Beloit College. Manger is the recipient of the Governor's Award in Support of the Arts for having founded Artists Working in Education Inc., a non-profit organization that provides meaningful art experiences in schools and parks for thousands of at-risk children.

Barbara Manger and her husband, Bill Lynch, live in Milwaukee, Wisconsin. They frequently travel to Wyoming to visit their son, Luke; his wife, Kathy; and their three grandsons.

CPSIA information can be obtained at www.ICGtesting.com
Printed in the USA
LVOW06s1432141113

361254LV00007B/96/P

9 780989 792318